MOVING TO A NEW LEVEL:
UNLEASHING GOD'S PURPOSE FOR YOUR LIFE

Dr. Rafael Osorio

Editorial Renovación
Wilbraham, MA, USA

July 2009

Moving to a New Level

Copyright © 2009 by Dr. Rafael Osorio.

Title of the original work in Spanish: Moviéndonos a un nuevo nivel
Copyright © 2006 by Dr. Rafael Osorio

Translation Team:	Lemuel González (Editor), Rafael Luis Osorio, Henry & Eliabelle Alicea, Oldelis Ramos, Eliel & Lisandra González
Cover Design:	Wilhem Morales

Editorial Renovación
P.O. Box 851
Wilbraham, MA 01095

Web site: www.EditorialRenovacion.com
E-mail: OsorioNewLevel@EditorialRenovacion.com

ISBN   978-0-9841009-0-3
LCCN   2009905816

Printed in the United States of America.

TABLE OF CONTENTS

DEDICATION

I want to dedicate my first book, first to my dear family composed of my beloved wife Loyda, my two children, Rafael Luis and Idaelis with her husband Lemuel, and my granddaughters, Kiana and Victoria.

This book is dedicated to my natural as well as spiritual parents: Rev. Luis Osorio and my mother Ana, who taught me from an early age about the love for God, His kingdom, the church, the ministry, and people. They also inculcated in me a love for music, reading, and composition in all its forms and expressions.

I also dedicate the book also to my beloved *Iglesia Apostólica Renovación* (Apostolic Renewal Church), starting with my pastors, the office personnel, and the church as a whole, that throughout these long years have moved bravely to new levels. They have paid the price and that is the reason why they now rejoice in the rewards that come from being obedient to the Lord. We are reaping as a church much of what was prophesied, but this has happened because there were those who believed the prophets and they were my beloved church.

I dedicate this book to all the pastors and churches that form the International Apostolic Renewal Network: to those in Peru, from Lima to the Amazon and all the beautiful pastors under the leadership of Apostle Víctor Salcedo and his wife Sonia; to those from San Rafael, Argentina with Pastor Antonio; to the brethren in Honduras with their Apostle Héctor Newman; to those in Puerto Rico, supervised by Pastor Henry Alicea, from Río Grande with Pastor Diny Osorio, my little sister, and all the way to the mountains of Corozal with pastors Víctor and Carmen Galí; and to those in the Dominican Republic with pastors Valentín and Raquel Rivera.

I also dedicate this to the pastors of the daughter churches in the United States: to Pastor Lilian Yvon in Holyoke, Massachusetts; Pastor Juanita Rosa in Stamford, Connecticut;

to the pastors Vida y Luis Gutierrez in Statesville, North Carolina; and to Pastor Amarilis Miralles, the wife of our dear friend Pastor Jose Miralles who is now with the Lord, in Hartford, Connecticut.

I also dedicate this book to the intercessors that the Lord has given me and my wife, not only in our church (prophets Marisol González, Maritza Ortega, Mariano Sanchez, Luis Lescano and the prayer warriors), but also to my intercessors in the nations, like Prophet Isidra del Orbe, Prophet Judith Yanira González, and to Prophet Ines Rivera, who is like a sister to me.

This book is dedicated to my spiritual mentors among them Apostle Alberto Guerrero from Chicago, and Hector Torres, a prophet to the nations, writer and teacher, who gave me the great privilege of ministering in the beautiful island of Cuba and taught me the first steps of the apostolic and prophetic dimension.

It is also dedicated to the collaborators in the ministry from whom I have also received much: Pastor Dr. David Remedios in Louisiana, who was the first to prophesy clearly about the coming new level for the church and for me; and from Puerto Rico Prophet Oscar Diaz, who opened doors in helping me organize our first Apostolic and Prophetic Conference.

Apostle-Pastor Dr. Rafael Osorio
November 2008

ACKNOWLEDGEMENTS

I thank my dear pastors Misael and Olga Ramos who took the task of editing the original text in Spanish and worked in the process of publishing the book. We have seen another dream come to pass.

I also thank my son-in-law, Lemuel González, for undertaking the effort to translate and edit this English version of the book. I offer my deepest gratitude to him and the entire translation team (my son Rafael Luis Osorio, Henry & Eliabelle Alicea, Oldelis Ramos, and Eliel & Lisandra González) who helped bring the vision to fruition. I also want to thank Wilhem Morales whose creative touch was vital in designing the book cover.

To all of you, my deepest thanks and above all to God be the glory. May the triune God receive all honor and exaltation forever and ever.

FOREWORD

During my travels over the last twelve years across Central, North and South America, and also Europe, Africa and the Caribbean, I have been able to see people of different cultural, social, and even religious backgrounds who share the same problem. That is the desire or impetus to want to improve, or even to come out of the painful situations in which they have been living for years, without being able to achieve their desires. In this book, we can find the answer to this problem through countless numbers of advice and guidance to drive and propel to a new level those who so desire.

Since I met Dr. Rafael Osorio a few years ago, I could see in him a deep knowledge and burden for the people he was serving, both locally and elsewhere, to change their lives in a positive way. Years later, I have seen the results in his church in Springfield and in the daughter churches around the world where I have been able to go with him to share the Word.

It fills me with joy to read and listen to the wisdom of this man, which over the years he has been able to accumulate, and now has been able to put all that experience and theological studies in this book to help many people move to new levels.

His sincerity, simplicity, and constant desire to serve the body of Christ with enthusiasm, has been a few of the many qualities that God has allowed me to see grow in such a short time in my spiritual son. He says in chapter 11 about faithfulness: "Anyone can be behind the scenes and serve, if the time is short. The challenge is to wait the necessary time doing what you are told, in a faithful and integral way. It is there where the heart of a faithful and loyal person is revealed."

In this book we can find extensive information that can be used as study material in a family group, Sunday school class, or even to prepare leaders. One of my favorite paragraphs is the prayers that Dr. Osorio makes for his readers and the prophetic statements he invites them to make. These can be found at the end of each chapter.

Good Stewardship and *Rest* are two chapters that have touched my life and ministry in a profound way, encouraging me to develop a better character and move to a new level. I have been able to see the results that these chapters have made in my life. I know that not only are the chapters mentioned above a blessing, but the others also; and I prophesy that your reading and study of this book will move you to a new level and expand your desire to continue serving in God's work.

Apostle Dr. Alberto Guerrero
May 2009

INTRODUCTION

This is a motivational, inspirational, and challenging book directed at people who, for different reasons, have been detained or stuck in their calling and purpose; when it is very much their time to advance to new levels and enter into their next season.

It is for the "Joshuas" of this time, who have received the command to cross over their "Jordan," but are still sitting waiting for their "Moses" to resurrect. This book is for the "Shulamites" of today who are still locked in their rooms with their winter clothes on, not knowing that winter has already passed, and the season of singing and flowers has come. It is directed to the different ministries that, like the people of Israel during exile, God had to send a prophet to announce to them to stop living and looking to the past. Soon He was about to do something new in their lives and they were running the risk of losing the opportunity, their "Kairos." That is why He tells them: "Rise up, and shine for your light has come, your time is here."

Throughout the different chapters, I identify some of the conditions and reasons that have caused many to remain stuck or detained, to turn back or to bypass their new season. In addition, I share some key strategies and steps to get out of this lethargy, understand the times of transition, and move forward with a firm step to a new level.

In Scripture, we see the concept of advancement and progress in all levels of life. For example:
- New levels of glory – Haggai: 2:9
- New levels of power – Psalm 84:7
- New levels of renewal and strength – 2nd Cor. 4:16
- New levels of the renewing of our minds – Romans 12:2
- New levels of perfection – Philemon 1:6, 1st Cor. 13:11
- New levels of revelation - Hebrews 5:11-14

I decided to write about this subject, because I have seen how we can be conformed and settle for the level that we have always been at, even when God is calling us to move forward. I have also seen how so many times, wanting to move and make the transition to a new time or season, we do not know how to do it. The time of transition is in itself a very difficult and challenging time, we might even say an intimidating time.

This has been a vital part of my experience particularly in the last few years, as an individual, leader, and a pastor for over 31 years. I am not writing from a rhetorical podium or academic perspective, but from my own experience. I had to confront fears, insecurities, criticism, impotence, loneliness, abandonment, and pain; in addition to the mistakes I made in the process of change and advancement. This has also been the experience of many leaders, pastors, and churches that I know. At the same time, thanks to God, I have had the opportunity of serving the Lord, shepherding many pastors and supervising ministries and churches. I have been able to share with them the insights that I share with you in this book, without ever wanting to suggest or imply that this book contains everything that is needed, or that it is the final word or authority on the subject.

It is time to advance, progress, and get ready for the next level of your divine calling. Moving to new levels implies a **change** of attitudes, thoughts, methods, relationships, vision, actions, and much more. Changing can be one of the most difficult experiences in life, but also one of the most gratifying. Let me clearly tell you: **without these changes, you will never advance in your calling. Do not fear change.**

My goal, when leaders and pastors read this book, is to motivate and challenge them in such a way that they do not retire or die taking with them their God-given dreams and visions, only because they did not know how to transition or feared to go to their new level. My desire and prayer is for you to rise up, initiate, press on, advance in your calling and ministry, and fulfill your purpose until the end; from stage to stage, level to level, from the current dimensions to new and greater dimensions, from glory to a greater glory.

I write against conformism, apathy, ritualism, the spirit of religiosity, fear, doubt, and previous failures that strike hundreds of pastors who have been wounded by their own churches, denominations, and spiritual children. I write against laziness, mediocrity, lack of vision, and the stubbornness of those who have taken the path of least resistance, and rather than conquering the obstacles in their lives, settle and only seek survival.

It is my prayer for you to rise up and cross your Jordan like **Joshua**; to come out of your locked room and enjoy your spring like the "Shulamite"; that you move from taking care of sheep to killing giants, from the desert to the palace like **David** and that you move from Moab to Bethlehem like **Ruth**.

I know there will be a price to pay; I can tell you now though that **it can be done and it is worth it.** I challenge you to advance to your new level and your new time. Make one of the mottos and inspiration of the Apostle Paul your own:

> "Forgetting what is behind, and straining for what
> is ahead, I press on toward the goal."
>
> Philippians 3:13

Shalom!

It's a New Season

Lyrics and music by Rev. Rafael Osorio

1

You hear a calling from the Spirit to the church
From the beloved to his bride, from the prophet to the people.
The time has come to rise up
To cross our Jordan and step on the Promised Land
No more excuses, it is time to advance,
Rise up, is the command of the Lord.

Chorus
It is a new time, time to advance,
Rise up, it's a new time,
Time of advancement, rise up,
It's a new time.

2

We come against fear and intimidation
That want to detain us and steal our moment.
No conformism and mediocrity
When God has told me to expand my wings.
No more excuses, it's time to advance,
Rise up, is the command of the Lord.

RISE UP

CHAPTER 1

"Moses My servant is dead.
Now therefore, arise, go over this Jordan ..."

Joshua 1:2

I like the first order God gives Joshua when his leader Moses dies: "Arise." This does not necessarily imply Joshua was physically sitting when God spoke to him; rather it refers to an attitude or a spiritual disposition. Sitting signifies being inactive, passive, without plans, and without an agenda. It is someone who has resigned to his circumstances, and is a spectator in the drama of his life.

No conqueror has won a battle sitting down; and no executive has catapulted their business to new levels with such an attitude. No one can prosper, be successful, and accomplish their purpose in life, if they are sitting.

> **If you want to move towards your new season, your new level, and your promotion in God, you must first rise up.**

God tells Joshua he would take on the task of completing Moses' mission: taking the people to the Promised Land and establishing them there. But He first says, "Arise." To cross the Jordan, set foot on the land, expel the enemies, and divide the inheritance, it was necessary in the first place that he rise up.

No one can undertake anything sitting down, tired, sleeping, fearful, or lazily. First, he must arise. Joshua had remained sitting contemplating the dead and old. The time of Moses had ended and the time of Joshua was starting, but he was sitting down (see Deuteronomy 31:7-8).

To stay seated next to what is dead and has ended is dangerous. To insist in flowing in things that have decayed or to sit next to what is dead is dangerous, because then we run the chance of dying as well; smelling rancid, like funeral flowers, like death. God had to repeat to Joshua what Moses had already told him: "It is your time, arise."

There are many people of God, next to their leaders, who are sitting before dead things, things that were effective and good in the past, but have ended, have reached their fulfillment, have simply died. Reviving what has already died and accomplished its task is pointless. It is time to rise up.

New times and seasons are received standing.

Arising is an attitude, primarily internally focused, an attitude of the spirit. It is believing in God, being ready, available, and prepared to accomplish the purpose of God. The great number of times the order "arise" appears in the Bible is a sign that it is a powerful and significant event and that something new is soon to begin. It is also the external sign, visible and physical, that indicates one season has ended and a new time begins.

Prodigal son: Luke 15:17-18

> "But when he came to himself, he said, 'How many of my father's hired servants have bread enough and to spare, and I perish with hunger! I will arise and go to my father ...."

When the younger son comes to grips with himself and his condition, he decides to return to his Father's house, where there is abundance. He decides to initiate the process of reconciliation and restoration and it all started with a war cry, with a change of attitude: "I will arise." Certainly, for the prodigal son his crying out "I will arise" meant he was tired of all the misery, scarcity, limitation, humiliation, and pain.

"I will arise" means the end of disobedience, arrogance, rebelliousness, waste, misery, poverty, of being among hogs and pods. It is the precursor to a new time; a new time where he reclaims his identity, his position, and his destiny. The father wanted to forgive him, dress him, and restore him as a son; but first the young man had to arise. Arising sets loose the rest of the process of restoration.

Paralytic in the Temple called Beautiful: Acts 3:3-6
"Who, seeing Peter and John about to go into the temple, asked for alms. And fixing his eyes on him, with John, Peter said, 'Look at us.' So he gave them his attention, expecting to receive something from them. Then Peter said, 'Silver and gold I do not have, but what I do have I give you: In the name of Jesus Christ of Nazareth, rise up and walk.'"

Peter gave an order to the paralytic man of many years who lived from the charity of people. Peter says: "Silver and gold I do not have, but what I do have I give you: In the name of Jesus Christ of Nazareth, rise up and walk." Verse five stands out for me, when the paralytic sees them arrive and makes his request, and he attentively waits to receive something from them.

This man was ready in his spirit to receive his new season. Physically he was sitting due to his condition, but in his spirit, he had already risen. It was almost as if he knew in his spirit that he would receive something so powerful that it would move him to a new season in his life. The time of misery, poverty, sickness, and pain was ending, and a new time of life, liberty, healing, and prosperity was beginning. Certainly, a new time in the life of this man began with Peter's order and with the obedience of a beggar.

Israel in the exile: Isaiah 60:1
"Arise, shine; for your light has come!
And the glory of the LORD is risen upon you."

The Prophet Isaiah orders the people of God in exile, in captivity, to arise and shine for their light has come, and the glory of the Lord has risen over them. The prophet is speaking, ordering, and prophesying over a new day, a new time for

Israel, a time of deliverance, of returning to their land and become a nation once more. He is prophesying over a new time of glory and splendor but it all begins with "**Arise.**"

It was imperative for the people to have a positive and faithful attitude in order to flow with their deliverance. It is the same for you now. First, you need to rise up, to proceed to your new level and time. Arise for your new time has come. Change your attitude and disposition.

Nehemiah and the leaders: Nehemiah 2:18

> "And I told them of the hand of my God which had been good upon me, and also of the king's words that he had spoken to me. So they said, 'Let us rise up and build.' Then they set their hands to this good work."

When Nehemiah reaches those remaining in Jerusalem, he finds them living among the ruble and in dishonor. He arrives and shares the vision God had given him to reconstruct the city. Instantly, those leaders capture the vision, and decide to make the vision a reality. It is then they say: "**Let us rise** and build."

We see in this example a change of attitude that provokes action. When Nehemiah arrives with the vision, the people were not waiting for him and less so to work in favor of his vision. Nehemiah had to first work with the passive and resigned attitude the people had adopted, to provoke in them an attitude of arising and overcoming.

The declaration "let us rise" indicated the time of inaction and of being spectators was reaching an end. The time of fear, conformity, passivity, and of sitting was reaching its end. "Let us rise" was the signal of a new season. It was the declaration of the arrival of a time of restoration and rebuilding.

The Beloved to the Shulamite: Song of Songs 2:10-13

> "My beloved spoke, and said to me:
> 'Rise up, my love, my fair one, and come away. For lo, the winter is past, the rain is over and gone. The

flowers appear on the earth; the time of singing has come, and the voice of the turtledove is heard in our land. The fig tree puts forth her green figs, and the vines with the tender grapes give a good smell. Rise up, my love, my fair one, and come away!'"

Why does the beloved tell the Shulamite to rise up? Because a new time for her life has come and he does not wish for her to miss her season. He tells her: "Rise up, my love, my fair one, and come away" because:

- Winter has passed; it has moved on,
- The rain has left,
- The flowers of the earth have appeared,
- The time of singing has come,
- The voice of the turtledove is heard in our land,
- The fig tree puts forth her green figs, and
- The vines with the tender grapes give a good smell.

There are seven reasons why the Beloved tells her: "Rise up, my love, my fair one and come away." I also declare these seven reasons for you. I prophetically announce in your favor that your time of winter has passed and a new season has arrived. Can you read over the seven reasons once more and tell yourself: these are seven reasons for which I will rise up in faith?

It is risky to remain sitting, lying down, disconnected, and unprepared when the time of the singing, of spring, of flowers, fig trees, and vines has come. We can let our best moment go by and lose a great opportunity while in such a negative state. We need to identify our spring season so we may arise, move, and enjoy it. The beloved does not want the Shulamite to miss that time and for that reason makes the calling: **"Rise up!"**

I want to tell you that your winter is about to end and your best time is about to begin. It is important you hear the calling of the Beloved to your life: **Rise up!** It is important you look out the window and see the rain has left, the trees have their leaves back, and the flowers are out. It is important to be able to smell the sweet aroma and perfume of the flowers and vines, and hear the song of the birds, their new accords and melodies of the new season. You have to shake loose, awaken, and rise up.

There are many with an attitude of remaining "seated" before their life due to the deceptions they have suffered or bad experiences, betrayal, failures, continual adversities or problems. They have decided to surrender and resign to their new time and their new spring. They have decided to live in a continuous winter. They have eliminated and disqualified themselves and say it's too late for me or it's not worth it now. On the contrary, I tell you today there is still hope: **Rise up!**

The case of Mephibosheth: 2nd Samuel 9:7-8

That is how David found Mephibosheth. He was a prince whom someone had dropped when he was small leaving him crippled. He had been left orphaned and alone. It appeared he would be forgotten and cast aside, and would live in pain and misery for the rest of his life. But to those depths David reached out searching for him to let him know his time of solitude, misery, and pain had reached their end.

David was announcing a new time for Mephibosheth. He recognized him as a prince, and would take him to his palace and permanently sit him at his table. David was going to take care of him, and assure he was respected and would lack nothing. Hallelujah! Certainly, a new time had reached this young man.

2nd Samuel 9:7

"So David said to him, 'Do not fear, for I will surely show you kindness for Jonathan your father's sake, and will restore to you all the land of Saul your grandfather; and you shall eat bread at my table continually.'"

Despite the initiative taken by King David, Mephibosheth had assumed a fatalist attitude towards himself and his life. He "sat" before his new time. We do not see him rejoicing with the news David brings or giving thanks for having been remembered. Mephibosheth gives David reasons for why he should let his new time pass by. He tells him he is not worth anything, that he is worse than a dead dog and his wish is to remain there in Lo Debar, which means a place of darkness, and not to go to the palace. Do you know anyone like that?

> "Then he [Mephibosheth] bowed himself, and said, What is your servant, that you should look upon such a dead dog as I?" 2nd Samuel 9:8

Sometimes the enemy does not need to attack us; since it turns out, we are our worst enemies. We are the ones who inflict the most damage on ourselves.

With that kind of attitude, Mephibosheth risked losing his opportunity. He had internalized a fatalistic attitude, one of resignation.

Now I move towards you in the same spirit as David, so you may shake loose the spirit of Mephibosheth and renounce all arguments and excuses, all deception, failure, depression, pain and bitterness, so that you may stand. I order you, in the name of the Lord, to rise up. There is a time of promotion from the valley of Lo Debar to the palace, to the King's table, from beggar to prince. God is an expert in effecting transitions in us. Psalm 113:5-9 says:

> "Who is like the LORD our God, who dwells on high, who humbles Himself to behold the things that are in the heavens and in the earth? He raises the poor out of the dust, and lifts the needy out of the ash heap, that He may seat him with princes — with the princes of His people. He grants the barren woman a home ..."

The Lord knows how to lift us up from the dust, from the ash heap, from the horrible pit, the miry clay, and place us among the princes of his people, and set our feet upon the rock.

I come to prophesize over you that you are like the prodigal son, who decided to return to his place of blessing.

That you will be like the paralytic of Acts 3 who was waiting to receive something powerful that could change him and his life. That you will be like the leaders of Jerusalem that captured Nehemiah's vision and moved from inertia to action. I declare that you will be like the Shulamite, who came out to see her spring and to intone a new song. Do not let the enemy steal your opportunity. This is your time! This is your new season!

- If you have passed through the winter, then you qualify for your spring.

- If you are living in Lo Debar, then you qualify for your palace.

- If you are living in scarcity, then you qualify for the abundance of the Father's house.

- Do not despise the Davids God sends to your Lo Debar to announce that a new time has come for you.

- Do not despise the Nehemiah who God sends your way while you are among the rubbles to announce that a new time has come.

- Do not despise your Beloved when he reaches your dark room, your dwelling place to announce the spring has arrived.

- Do not despise the very voice of God, through the Holy Spirit, that tells you as he told Joshua: Arise.

Brother, leader, beloved pastor; rise up, shake loose and change your attitude, change your disposition! Your ministry is going to a new time, to a new level. Are you willing to flow with God or will you let the opportunity pass you by?

- Church rise up! Once and for all, leave the rubble of tradition and of those religious practices that are ineffective.

- Church rise up and leave your Lo Debar. Come out of all darkness, since it is time to shine.

- Church rise up and leave the pig's pen and the level of eating pods and find your place in the Father's House; recoup your position, identity, vision, and provision.

- Church rise up and take your winter coats off since it is now spring.

- Church rise up and change your lamenting for a song of life, happiness, and power. Let go of the spirit of Mephibosheth. Remember you are a chosen generation, a royal priesthood, and a holy nation.

- Church rise up, and let go of the shackles of captivity and let us take possession of the land the Lord has given us.

Rise up!   Rise up!   Rise up!

If you want to advance to the new time and to your new level: Rise up! It is an order from the Lord.

My Prayer

Lord, I pray that my dear readers may shake loose all inertia, passivity, conformism, excuses, arguments, and that they may stand up.

I pray that they do not let their opportunities, their new time, pass them by, and that they may hear the voice of the Holy Spirit that says: "Rise up!" We activate the Joshuas of this time who need to arise to cross the Jordan and in so doing conquer their dreams and visions. We rebuke every spirit of Mephibosheth at this time, so that we may leave Lo Debar and direct our steps towards the palace. We leave the pods to sit at the table of the King and Heavenly Father.

I pray so that all negative attitudes of complaining, lamenting, murmuring, and accusations cease. That my dear reader may take his harp and begin to intone the song of the spring, a song of praise to God, of faith, victory, and new beginnings.

I pray so at this time each pastor, each leader, each ministry, and every church may rise up. So they may not lose their new time, but rather begin to walk in it. In Christ Jesus, we pray. Amen.

My Prophetic Declaration

- I declare my new time has come and I will not let it go by.

- I declare I will rise up in faith with a new attitude and disposition.

- I declare I will let go of my winter coat, which is my lament and complaint.

- I declare I will leave my hiding place of rubbles, of pig's pen, and of Lo Debar.

- I declare this is my spring season, of being in the palace and of restoration.

- I declare it is my time of promotion.

- I declare the time of my song has come and in obedience to the Beloved, I rise up and move in faith. Amen.

INITIATE

CHAPTER 2

"… do not turn from it to the right hand or to the
left, that you may prosper wherever you go."
                                            Joshua 1:7b

I n order to move into a new time you first need to have the
correct attitude and disposition and only then can you
begin to take the first steps to initiate what God has
ordained for you to do. I want to speak to you about the
importance of that first step. I want to speak to you about the
power there is in people who embark on their journey, in
people who take initiative, people who know how to provoke
their blessings and move the hand of God upon their lives.

As soon as God asked Joshua to stand up and gave him
the divine agenda, He said to him:

> "Only be strong and very courageous, that you may
> observe to do according to all the law which Moses
> My servant commanded you; do not turn from it to
> the right hand or to the left, that you may prosper
> wherever you go."   Joshua 1:7

God was saying to his servant: I am going to endorse
you, I am going to bless you, and I am going to provide for
you. God was telling him that he was personally going to take
care of him so he may have success in what he was ordered to
do. You have to give life to the vision. In other words, the
Lord was saying to him, I will bless, prosper, and endorse you
as you initiate what I have ordered you to do.

It is important to understand the order. First God told
Joshua to start, and then God would prosper him. It is here
where many are held back. They have inverted the order of

things; they are first waiting for prosperity, provision, and the victory of God to act.

> **There are many waiting for God, but in reality, God is waiting for many.**

To move and flow in the new time you have to take the first step. You have to start and initiate what God has ordained you to do. I think the biggest potential for failure we face is to pass through our lives without daring to initiate anything, especially, our dreams and visions. The problem of many is ignorance. They say they do not know what God has for them, they lack dreams and visions, and for this reason, they cannot initiate them.

Fear of Failure

The problem with others is not the lack of revelation or information, but an issue with action. It is the fear of failing, fear of being wrong, fear of not finishing projects, fear of lacking resources, fear that no one endorses them or that they will be abandoned, fear of not measuring up to people's expectations, fear of criticism, and fear that their image and reputation is affected. Fear, fear, fear. Because of the fear of failure, they do not get started on anything. To flow in your new time you have to be able to risk getting out of your comfort zone.

The Duke of Wellington declared many years ago: "The only thing I am afraid of is fear."[1] John Maxwell, warning about the power of fear says: "If allowed to control our lives, fear can be a permanent detour on the success journey, stopping us from making any progress."[2]

I sincerely believe it is better to fail at doing something, undertaking what God has placed in your heart, than to fail by not trying and missing opportunities. In fact, the only people who have not experienced failure are the ones who have never tried to win at anything. There is no worse epitaph than this one:

"Never failed, but never tried anything. Never obtained a loss, but never tasted victory."

"If you want to continue on the success journey, you need to learn to fail forward. When you have the right attitude, failure is neither fatal nor final. In fact, it can be a springboard to success."[3]

As the writer John Ortberg delineates in his book by the same title: "If you want to walk on water, you have to get out the boat."[4] We criticize Peter for sinking in the waters after firmly walking on them, but we never criticize the eleven fear-filled disciples who failed by not getting out of the boat. President John F. Kennedy said: "There are risks and costs to action. But they are far less than the long range risks of comfortable inaction."[5]

A critic of Thomas A. Edison said to him: "Do you not get tired of failing? You have more than 1900 failed attempts." Edison answered: "I have not failed 1900 times; I just discovered 1900 ways not to create the light bulb." Edison was saying, I am learning from my trials and because I am learning I am growing, therefore, those so called failed attempts are not really failures.[6] We can learn, grow, mature, and expand even from failures.

There are people who use their failures as burial stones, but others use them as stepping stones to ascend to their next level. "Failure isn't failure unless you don't learn from it."[7] Don't you find it interesting the way God reveals himself in Psalm 146:7-8?

"... The LORD gives freedom to the prisoners. The LORD opens *the eyes of* the blind; The LORD raises those who are bowed down ..."

We should not be afraid to begin the things God has sent us to do because if we fail in the attempt we have the promise that "... he raises those who are bowed down..." Hallelujah!

> If you have fallen or have failed, then you qualify to be lifted up by God so that you return to the sphere of action.

Slothfulness

Another reason that impedes many from taking that first step is slothfulness. Speaking clearly, some people are simply lazy. They do not want to put out any effort, invest energy, money, time, and resources into things. They want the results and vision, but they want others to obtain it for them.

How many ask for prayer and fasting in their favor! But they do not even come to the prayer service or the fasting events to intercede for their own lives. Many people want to be educated and be in a better financial position. However, they do not search for a job and if they have a job, they are mediocre workers; they do everything that would qualify them to be fired. Look at what Proverbs 13:4 says:

> "The soul of a lazy man desires [has vision], and has nothing [lacks action-inactivity]; But the soul of the diligent [starters] shall be made rich." [Comments added]

God's commitment is with the diligent, people who start things and people who work. If some are not willing to invest in their dreams and visions, then God will not invest in them. Suppose two young people come to me asking for financial support to go to school, then after one week, I find one sitting down in a sofa eating popcorn and watching television while the other one is coming from an orientation at a college. Whom do you think I am going to sponsor? As it was once well said by Vince Lombardi: "The dictionary is the only place that success comes before work."[8]

In order to move to a new time you have to get rid of the spirit of weakness, slothfulness, and vacationing 24/7. The ones who qualify for a Sabbath are those who have worked during the week. There are people who have six days of

Sabbath and one day of work, and even then, they are absent that one day of work because they are tired.

Spectators

Others have come to be spectators of their own lives. What do I mean? Their life is like going to the movie theater, and sitting idly down to watch a movie about their own life without having an opinion over the scenes or the screenplay. They accept everything that happens in their lives without any standards or criteria. Meanwhile, others have decided to be the main actor and protagonist of their lives. They are brave and ask the director for the script so that they can rewrite it or add their touch. They make changes, intervene, act, initiate, and provoke.

Jabez

This is the case with Jabez. He did not like the story of his life. He did not accept the curse or backwardness cast upon his life. Jabez dared to rewrite the script of his life. He initiated changes; he dared to pray to God for His blessings, the deliverance of all curses, and the expansion of his territory.

> "And Jabez called on the God of Israel saying, 'Oh, that You would bless me indeed, and enlarge my territory, that Your hand would be with me, and that You would keep *me* from evil, that I may not cause pain!' So God granted him what he requested."
>
> 1st Chronicles 4:10

He did not wait for anyone or for a prophet; he took the initiative. The last part of that verse says God granted him what he had requested. God prospered him and he was more illustrious than his brothers were.

There are people waiting for their circumstances to change by themselves. They are waiting for everyone else to approve of them to begin to act, to take that first step. They are waiting for their giant to die, their mountain to move, and their storm to change paths all by themselves.

Saul, David and Goliath

This was the case of King Saul and his army as they faced the Philistines and Goliath, the giant. They were in the place of combat. They had soldiers, weapons, and enemies; all of the necessary ingredients for war. Nevertheless, they did not initiate the battle. They did not surrender or return home, but they also never took action. They were waiting for the giant to get tired, go home, or even die of a heart attack while waiting on the sidelines.

In contrast, there are people, like David, who make things happen; they set in motion events that cause the hand of God to move. What a difference in attitude in the face of adversity before the giant Goliath!

> "Then David said to Saul, 'Let no man's heart fail because of him; your servant will go and fight with this Philistine.'"
>
> 1st Samuel 17:32

> "Then David said to the Philistine, 'You come to me with a sword, with a spear, and with a javelin. But I come to you in the name of the LORD of hosts, the God of the armies of Israel, whom you have defied. This day the LORD will deliver you into my hand, and I will strike you and take your head from you. And this day I will give the carcasses of the camp of the Philistines to the birds of the air and the wild beasts of the earth, that all the earth may know that there is a God in Israel.'"
>
> 1st Samuel 17:45-46

Goliath was defeated because the Spirit of God came over David. The Spirit of the Lord came over him because he initiated the attack, and took the first step, the one that Saul never took. Remember the biblical principle: "You will prosper in those things that you start."

It is time for your first step, to overcome fear, to come out of slothfulness, to leave your comfort zone. It is time to confront your circumstances, and to move to your new level.

> **Your new level is only a step away.**
> **The rest of the steps are waiting for the first.**

"The most important thing is to begin, even though the first step is the hardest."[9]

There are things that are not going to come about, take form until you take that first step. I am specifically referring to those things that are God's will for your life. God's beautiful and anointed plans for your life are going to stay in a *potential* state until you take the first step.

It is not enough to be pregnant with the visions and dreams. In its due time, you have to push and you have to give birth. It is not enough to be a visionary or a dreamer; you have to be an initiator and a starter. You have to put flesh, hands, feet, and life to the vision. God is waiting for us to believe Him and start our calling to bless us and open a way, doors, resources, miracles, signs, wonders, and victories.

Moses in front of the Red Sea

In the passage that narrates the event where Moses and the people are in front of the Red Sea while they were fleeing from the Pharaoh's army, God, for the first time, interrupts a prayer service to say it is not time to pray, it is time to act. God did not want another prayer; he wanted action. There is nothing more powerful than prayer, but many times, we use prayer to stop and delay the action. We can utilize prayer as a mechanism to postpone the things we have to do. Do you know people like that? People who are always praying and praying for a project, plans, or decisions to be made, but in reality prayer is a form of justification of their inaction, of postponing their decision making process and the moment of facing their reality. You will never be able to move to your new level, if you are always delaying things. "About the only thing that comes to a procrastinator is old age."[10] There are leaders who have been in front of the Red Sea for years while the staff is at their side.

"And the LORD said to Moses, 'Why do you cry to Me? Tell the children of Israel to go forward. But lift up your rod, and stretch out your hand over the sea and divide it. And the children of Israel shall go on dry ground through the midst of the sea.'"

Exodus 14:15-16

Do you know why Moses did not have to pray at that moment? He did not have to pray because the waters of the Red Sea were ready for him. What he needed to do was to extend his staff, give the order and the miracle would happen. As soon as Moses initiated it, the sea had to divide. Every march is started with the first step. Repeat it to yourself: it is time to march, to advance to my new season.

Joshua and the waters of the Jordan

The people and Joshua also crossed the waters of the Jordan the same way. The waters of the Jordan were waiting for the feet of the priest.

"... and as those who bore the ark came to the Jordan, and the feet of the priests who bore the ark dipped in the edge of the water (for the Jordan overflows all its banks during the whole time of harvest), that the waters which came down from upstream stood still, and rose in a heap very far away at Adam, the city that is beside Zaretan. So the waters that went down into the Sea of the Arabah, the Salt Sea, failed, and were cut off; and the people crossed over opposite Jericho."

Joshua 3:15-16

What would have happened if the priest waited for the waters to recede?

I want to prophesy that your Jordan is waiting for your feet, for that first step. It is time for you to take your first step. Loosen that first step; take up the spirit of initiative. Start what God has spoken over your life. Take out the visions, plans that you have put away, renounced, and forgotten. Heaven is waiting for you, as Matthew 18:18 says.

> "Assuredly, I say to you, whatever you bind on earth
> will be bound in heaven, and whatever you loose on
> earth will be loosed in heaven."

Whatever you bind and loose here on earth will be bound and loose in heaven. You initiate here on earth, where you have circumstantiates and trials and heaven acts and sets them loose. There are angels waiting for you. There are provisions and miracles waiting for you. There is prosperity, sponsorship, favor, and provision from God waiting for you.

The windows of heaven are ready to open and liberate blessings until they are overflowing for your life but they are waiting for your tithes. Your *bringing* liberates the *opening* according to Malachi 3:10

> "'Bring all the tithes into the storehouse, that there
> may be food in My house, and try Me now in this,'
> says the LORD of hosts, 'If I will not open for you the
> windows of heaven and pour out for you such blessing
> that there will not be room enough to receive it.'"

Jesus said that those who want to receive would first have to ask, those who want to find, would first have to seek, and those who want to come in, would first have to knock. This is a very clear message.

> "Ask, and it will be given to you; seek, and you will
> find; knock, and it will be opened to you. For
> everyone who asks receives, and he who seeks finds,
> and to him who knocks it will be opened."
> Matthew 7:7-8

I like people who provoke blessings. People who are not waiting for their circumstances to change so they can begin things. Paul and Silas did something unusual as their imprisonment lingered until the midnight hour. At midnight, they began to sing hymns and pray to God. They set loose an earthquake that freed them from prison and provoked the salvation of the jailer, his family, and the establishment of a powerful church in the city. What would have happened if they had not done what they did? (Acts 16:25-34)

Let us take the case of Bartimaeus when he learned that Jesus was passing by. Notice that Bartimaeus initiated the miracles with his shouting. Despite of not knowing Jesus, not being in Jesus' agenda, being blind, a beggar, being one person in the midst of many, and having a group of people who opposed him from getting help, Bartimaeus took the first step and made Jesus stop and minister to him. What would have happened if Bartimaeus had kept his mouth shut? (Mark 10:46-52)

What would have happened?

What would have happened if the woman who had a flow of blood for twelve years had not taken the first step and dragged herself through the pressing crowd to draw virtue from Jesus by touching him? What would have happened if Zacchaeus had not climbed the tree to see Jesus? What would have happened if the paralytic of Capernaum had not decided that with his friends they would break the ceiling and get to the place where Jesus was? What would have happened if the Canaanite woman would have left Jesus and not asked for the health of her daughter? What would have happened if Queen Esther had not bravely entered into the king's chamber to intercede? What would have happened if Jabez had not prayed they way he did? What would have happened?

> **What will happen to you if you
> do not take the first step?**

It is time to leave the excuses behind and begin to take action. Stop saying: "I don't take the first step because no one helps me, no one understands me, I don't have anything, I don't know, I am a woman, or I am a single mother." Stop justifying your inaction by saying: "I am Hispanic, I am dark skinned, I am poor, I live in the city or in the country, the economy is bad, I have a past, because my parents were absent, because the ones I love betrayed me, I was abused, it's too hot, too cold, too dark, too dangerous, no one has done this before, etc, etc, etc."

Personal Testimonies of the First Step

I remember that a few years ago our church was interested in purchasing the house adjacent to our sanctuary. We prayed concerning this purchase for some time, but the price was too high for us to buy it, some one hundred ten thousand dollars. The house had two levels, many rooms, bathrooms, and parking. It was in good condition. At some point, I was informed that price had dropped and the house was being sold for forty-five thousand dollars. That is when we intensified our prayers, especially in the morning hours and we sealed it with a march around the block and surrounded the house to claim it. Nevertheless, not everyone thought that we could purchase it because we did not have the money. A church official reminded me that we did not have that amount of money in the budget and that it would be impossible to gather the money to buy the house.

Some time later, I met with a real estate agent and made an offer of thirty thousand dollars, thought to be a ridiculous offer. Surprisingly, the owners accepted the offer. We had to come up with ten thousand dollars for the down payment and three hundred dollars a month for eight years for the mortgage payment. We did not have the ten thousand dollars for the down payment, but I had already taken that first step. In that meeting with the realtor, a leader said to me "count on me for five thousand dollars," while another said "count on me for two thousand."

That night, when I communicated everything to the church, in the prayer service, we collected three thousand dollars, the rest of the money we needed for the down payment. In addition, some brethren promised to give three hundred dollars a month to pay for the loan. The pledges added up to nine hundred dollars a month. That night we rejoiced in the Lord for His provision. At the end, we were able to pay the house in two years. It was a process of faith and prayer, but it was the first step that released the rest of the miracles. When we took the first step, God prospered us. I did not wait for the ten thousand to arrive, but instead my first step released the money needed.

In another occasion, God brought us to the Dominican Republic to start a mission and support certain churches in that country. I decided to bring a group of young people with me to help me with the music, worship, and work with the children. Some of the parents decided to do fundraising activities to purchase the plane tickets. However, on the day that they began to prepare the food for the fundraiser everything went wrong.

Some parents did not arrive, others did not bring what was asked of them, the work doubled, and anxiety and frustration settled in. When I went to the kitchen one of the parents said to me: "Pastor, this is impossible, we will never be able to raise the money in three months and we cannot buy them because we don't have the money. It's better to cancel the trip." Can you imagine how I felt, but I said: "the trip is on, God is going to provide, and He is going to be glorified. The money is there."

Immediately I went home, I locked myself in the room of the basement and I prayed to God. I presented the issues and claimed the money. The next day, on Sunday, while we were in worship, I was playing the keyboard and a young adult said to me in the ear: "I have received some money from a settlement; I have brought with me $2,500 as a gratitude offering. Where should I put the money? Tell me and I will do it." I almost fell off the keyboard chair. Recovering my breath I said, "put it in missions for the missionary trip to the Dominican Republic."

That first step, believing God would provide and pressing on with the project, liberated God's prosperity and provision. Even though the money was not there yet, the fundraising activity was a failure, and the parents were skeptical, I took the first step. We began the project and God prospered us. I did not wait for the $2,500 to start planning the trip; my first step liberated the rest.

Time for Action

It is time to act. It is time to begin the great things God has prepared for you, your family, your ministry, and your church. Pastors, it is time to initiate dreams and visions that are in your heart. It is time to march and place your feet upon the waters that separate you from your divine destiny. Do not stop anymore. It is time to advance! Church it is time to move forward.

- It is time to scream like Bartimaeus.

- It is time for you to drag yourself and press through the crowd like the woman who had a flow of blood for twelve years.

- It is time to climb the tree like Zacchaeus.

- It is time to break the ceiling that separates you from your blessings like the paralytic of Capernaum.

- It is time to walk towards the Father's house as the prodigal son did.

- It is time to remove all the ashes and force your hands like the leaders under Nehemiah.

- It is time to pray like Jabez.

Pastor Tony Miller expresses it very clearly: "When your determination to get up and go forward is stronger than your fear of failure or the nagging obstacles that seek to hinder your trip, your adventure toward significance will begin."[11]

Your new time awaits your first step. Initiate, start, act now.

Chapter 2 Notes

(1) <u>Your Road Map for Success: You Can Get There from Here</u> - John Maxwell – Thomas Nelson 2002 (p. 120)

(2) <u>Your Road Map for Success: You Can Get There from Here</u> - John Maxwell - Thomas Nelson 2002 (p. 121)

(3) <u>Your Road Map for Success: You Can Get There from Here</u> - John Maxwell - Thomas Nelson 2002 (p. 128)

(4) <u>If You Want To Walk On Water, You Have To Get Out The Boat</u>- John Ortberg - Zondervan 2001 (p. 7)

(5) <u>Your Road Map for Success: You Can Get There from Here</u> - John Maxwell - Thomas Nelson 2002 (p. 121)

(6) <u>Think on these Things</u> - John Maxwell - Beacon Hill Press 1999 (p. 90)

(7) <u>Your Road Map for Success: You Can Get There from Here</u> - John Maxwell - Thomas Nelson 2002 (p. 146) Cita del Dr. Ronald Niednagel

(8) Quote attributed to Vince Lombardi.

(9) <u>Imitation is limitation</u> - John Mason – Bethany House Publishers 2004 (p. 41)

(10) <u>Imitation is limitation</u> - John Mason - Bethany House Publishers 2004 (p. 118)

(11) <u>Journey to Significance</u> – Tony Miller – Charisma House 2003 (p. 3)

My Prayer

Lord, I ask you to bless my beloved readers giving them strength to initiate what they should have initiated before. I release in them an initiating spirit. I declare that they will move from being a spectator on the sidelines to initiating, from slothfulness to action. I pray they would rid themselves of all excuses, arguments, and justification that impedes their initiating. I cast out all slothfulness and fear.

I order them to begin their march to place their feet in their Jordan. I pray that they will not die without achieving their potential and that they will activate their potential trusting that whatever they initiate will prosper as you have promised. In Christ Jesus, we pray. Amen.

My Prophetic Declaration

- I declare this is a season to take my first step; it is my time to initiate my walk towards my destiny.

- I declare it is my time to march.

- I declare it is my time to initiate the dreams, visions, and projects God has placed in me.

- I declare I am as Joshua, Bartimaeus, Jabez, Paul, and Silas. I declare I will not sit around waiting for my circumstances to change, but I will change my circumstances. I provoke my blessing and God's hand of blessing upon me. I boldly ask, knock, search, and initiate.

- I declare that my steps of faith and action release the prosperity of God in my life, family, and ministry. Amen.

PRESS ON

CHAPTER 3

*"... But one thing I do, forgetting those things which
are behind and reaching forward to those things
which are ahead, I press toward the goal ..."*
Philippians 3:13-14

This is the third motivational motto for anyone who desires to reach their new season: Press on! Arise! Initiate! Press on! This is the maxim for those who have started on their vision, for those who have taken off from the starting line, because he who has not begun anything cannot press on. This is also the theme of those who have not reached the finish line, their destiny; those who have not reached their new level. One thing is to begin something and it is another to finish it.

> **Between the beginning and the end is the pressing on.**

Your first step is followed by pressing on. Pressing on is the shout of victory of those who know they have not arrived yet, but are determined to reach their goal. Are you determined to reach your goal? The Apostle Paul was determined to reach his goal. That is why in Philippians 3:13 he says: "One thing I do, one thing I go after and that is to press on to reach my goal." Only those people who are determined to reach their goal will press on.

Pressing on is in the minds and hearts of people who are in transit, moving towards their goal. They are those who are still in the valley, but know that where they really want to be is at the summit and that is why they press on, because they have not reached it yet. They do as Psalms 84:6-7 says, they cross the valley:

"As they pass through the Valley of Baca, they make it a spring; the rain also covers it with pools. They go from strength to strength; each one appears before God in Zion *[the summit]*."

A traveler who is required to stop at a different country while on his way to his final destination is often referred to as a stopover passenger, because even when the traveler arrives to an intermediary country, it is not his final destination. This traveler will continue on his journey. Other travelers will leave the airport, but the stopover passengers do not leave their gate, they do not go to find their luggage nor call their relatives to pick them up, because they know they are in transit, they have not yet arrived, and they must press on.

You cannot be confused with the places you must pass through believing you have reached your goal. You cannot negotiate with these places and make a permanent housing in places that are transitory. It is vital to remain firm before the opposition or the difficulty and never decide to stop half way toward your destination.

I know people who instead of pressing on, crossing their valley, and reaching their goal, decide to stay half way to their destination. They embarked on their journey, they are not in the valley, but they did not reach the summit either. They are not doing poorly, they are doing good things, but they missed the excellent. They remained half way to their destination.

Many people start many things, but few finish. The problem for them is not initiating projects. Their major problem is pressing on until they are finished. Do you know people like that? Half way through their goal, instead of pressing on, they abandon their current project for a new project. They give up instead of pressing on. They go back to school, invest in tuition, buy the books, uniform and transportation, but before the year is over, they withdraw. They become members of a sports team and buy all the equipment, they go to the practices, but before the end of the season and tournaments, they stop going.

You go to their houses and see in every corner things that have been forgotten or are now without use; things like the once exciting exercise equipment and gym clothes that are probably even brand name clothes, and the gym membership, that even though it is paid for it has not been used for six months. They bought the <u>Inglés sin Barreras</u> English study program and you can see that the majority of the videos are still new in their original box. You can see the <u>MasterLife</u> discipleship books out in a corner, because they just started the weekly classes again for a third time and it has been two weeks since the last class they attended. Maybe they got an extra job or a little overtime on Tuesday nights and forgot all about their existing commitment to the discipleship classes on that same night. Do you know people like that?

It is surprising to see the great number of people who are constantly celebrating, from party to party, when nothing has been finished or accomplished; celebrating without cause, without reaching their goal, and wasting time instead of pressing on. Many might think, judging by the amount of parties some of them attend, that they have gotten ahead a lot and reached many victories and success. However, especially in our Hispanic culture, the reality is that those who celebrate the most and attend parties are those who really do not have a reason to celebrate. Those who arrive at the party first are those who withdrew from school, those who failed, those who lost their job for having many absences or a bad attitude, those who have some kind of addiction or are lazy, and simply sleep and eat a lot.

I am not talking about getting rid of an enthusiastic, happy and positive attitude, but I cannot agree with an agenda filled with parties and celebrations when it is time to press on. I believe in celebrations and parties, but in their due time, when there is good reason to celebrate. When one reaches one's goals or at least major milestones, where one can make a stop to celebrate the progress made and reward one self. Those kinds of parties serve as a motivation and not a delay. Paul writes these words to Timothy:

"The hardworking farmer must be first to partake of the crops."   2nd Timothy 2:6

There are people who want to celebrate as if it were the time of the harvest without having sown anything. That time should instead be invested nurturing, feeding, watering, and taking care of the crop. That goes first, and later you can call a party and enjoy the fruits of the harvest. This is the same message found in Psalm 126:5-6:

> "Those who sow in tears shall reap in joy. He who continually goes forth weeping, bearing seed for sowing, shall doubtless come again with rejoicing, bringing his sheaves with him."

Everything has its season. Everything has its time. There is a time for working, pressing on, and also a time to enjoy and celebrate.

The father of the prodigal son did not party every day. He celebrated when his lost son was found. We have to be careful with procrastination, entertainment, and parties here and there, when we should be spending our time pressing on toward the goal. Proverbs 6:6-11 gives us a warning.

> "Go to the ant, you sluggard! Consider her ways and be wise, which, having no captain, overseer or ruler, provides her supplies in the summer, and gathers her food in the harvest. How long will you slumber, O sluggard? When will you rise from your sleep? A little sleep, a little slumber, a little folding of the hands to sleep— so shall your poverty come on you like a prowler, and your need like an armed man."

Although in this case the reason for the failure or not reaching the goal is laziness, it is important to notice that it has the same effect as those who are constantly from party to party. The ant presses on in her work, even if the summer comes.

During the time Puerto Rico was a Spanish colony, a Spanish governor came up with a strategy to continue controlling the people and keeping them from rebelling against the Spanish empire. This governor called his strategy the plan of the 3 Ds: Drinking, Dancing, and a Deck of Cards. He said: "If we give the people these three things, if we keep them in a spirit of celebration and dancing, they will never rebel, they will stay where they are and we will continue in power." The devil still uses this strategy to keep us from reaching our goals, to keep us from pressing on to our next level. The plan is to drug us, entertain us, and distract us to keep us from pressing on. This is the reason why many people do not wait for Friday night or the weekend to celebrate. Now, many begin partying on Thursday and others do it every day of the week.

As a pastor, I am not pleased by those brethren who only come to church when there is party, food, gifts, and refreshments. I call them the "Koinonia" brethren. However, they never come to their <u>MasterLife</u> discipleship classes or the yearly church clean up, nor do they help a family in need. Do you know people like that?

I remember in particular a family who, at the beginning of my ministry in Springfield, would come to the services two or three times a year, but somehow the whole family was always present at the Christmas party. Even though it had been months since they attended their last service, somehow they knew when the date of the party was and would come. They would sit on the front row, and would greet everyone like nothing had happened and they had been there all along. They would eat like someone who had been fasting for two days, and they would even bring containers to take leftovers home.

> **Adopt the motto of the Apostle Paul: "one thing I do, I press on towards the goal." Do not allow anything or anyone to stop or distract you.**

Many times when someone initiates a project, a new business or job, there is an inauguration or a kick-off event. It is a happy, positive, and enthusiastic event. Important people attend and come to motivate and wish the best for that enterprising person. In the same manner, when you are reaching the finish line of a race towards your victory, there are many people waiting for you at the finish line. Photos are taken. There are reporters, flowers, trophies, colors, music, etc. But dear friend, the hardest and most challenging time is in the middle of the race. Remember: between the beginning and the end is the "pressing on."

The time to press on is not as popular as the beginning or end of something. During this time, the number of people who remain by your side, motivating and helping you decreases greatly. During this time, there are no photos or music. There are no articles or celebrations. It is a difficult time. It is a time of hard work, of making crucial decisions, of facing obstacles and problems. In the beginning and the end, the day is "sunny," but when you are pressing on, not every day will be sunny: cloudy days will come and even more stormy days will come your way.

Remember that between Egypt and the Promise Land there was a desert. Do you understand what I am talking about? It is in the desert where many give up as they face the difficulty of crossing, of pressing on. It is here where Paul says; "One thing I do: I press on." It is impossible to move to the new season without pressing on.

> I congratulate you for getting up, for arising. I congratulate you for embarking towards your dreams and visions, for taking the first step. Now it is time to press on.

To press on you have to learn how to establish a relationship with your past, present, and future. Pressing on will depend on how you relate with your past life, your future life, and of course, your current life. Read Philippians 3:13-14 once more.

Past

Paul said, that in order to press on we first must forget what lies behind; our past. You will not press on to your new time without relating correctly with your past. Your past can stop you or can propel you towards your new time. Certainly, the emotional chains of your past could be as powerful as real chains. If you are in chains or bondage, it will be difficult to advance.

This was the reason why the Lord, speaking through the prophet, orders the people in exile not to remember the past anymore.

> "Do not remember the former things, nor consider the things of old. Behold, I will do a new thing, now it shall spring forth; shall you not know it? I will even make a road in the wilderness and rivers in the desert."
>
> Isaiah 43:18-19

If they remained focused on their past, they were not going to be able to discern the new time the Lord prepared for them. They ran the risk of losing their "kairos" because their mind, sight and heart were dominated by the memory of the past thereby impeding them from becoming pregnant with the vision of God. There is an order to refocus or redirect your sights towards the future, towards the "it shall spring forth." There is an order to lift your eyes with expectations versus an attitude of resignation, conformance, and passivity.

If we allow it, the past has the power to destroy the future. The past has the power to relegate us to the desert, even if there is a new path where previously there was none. It also has the power to limit us to the barren land, when there are rivers that are fertilizing the earth that awaits us. We do not realize it because we turn our face away.

Many do not move to their next level because their memories are filled with failures, errors, and painful experiences and they do not have room for new thoughts of victory. No one can advance to his or her new time with an inconsistent sight: sometimes looking ahead and other times looking behind. Lot's wife gives us the best example showing us this duality does not work and the only thing it will produce is to leave us half way between Sodom and Gomorrah. When our sight is concentrated in what we have left behind, we run the danger of turning into pillars of salt half way to our new level. Believe me; the phenomenon of turning into a salt pillar as Lot's wife did is still happening today. There are many pillars of salt nowadays.

> For many people, the painful experiences and failures of the past explain their present and their opportunities. Their traumatic experiences are the ones governing their lives. These experiences call the shots and run the show in their lives.

I ask you, does your past determine if you are qualified for a task? Does your past determine if you are capable, if your deserve it or not? Is bitterness, rejection, failure, abuse, and humiliation the stronger voice in you?

Paul says with certainty that he had to forget his past, that which lied behind. The past is in the past. We cannot change anything about it. However, our future it is yet to be written. To forget and leave behind our past does not mean we get amnesia or deny what happened. To forget simply means to dethrone the past of any decisive power over your life. It is the action of unmasking the past and conquering over it.

> **Remember: That which you do not conquer, will conquer you.**

To forget is to go through the healing of our wounds. Wounds are healed, and though there is a scar or mark left, no infection or pain remains. To forget is to be free from the traumatic effects of the experiences in our past.

Joseph

Joseph, Jacob's son, was sold by his brothers and became a slave in the land of Egypt. Later in life, he had two sons. The first he named Manasseh, which means "God has made me forget all my trouble and all my father's household." The second he called Ephraim, which means "God has made me fruitful in the land of my suffering." (Genesis 41:50-52). An interesting dynamic is at play in the naming of the two sons. They show the process of healing and victory Joseph experienced to fulfill God's calling in his life.

Think about everything Joseph went through because of his brothers. He had to deal with much pain. The pain is magnified when inflicted by those we love the most and we hope would do us well. He had to deal with bitterness, anger, resentfulness, thoughts of vengeance, and depression, among others. Finally, with God's help, Joseph was able to forget. In other words, Joseph received healing and divine ointment upon his life, even though he did not know if he would get to see his brothers again.

After he forgives his brothers and everyone who had caused him harm, his second son is born, Ephraim: God has made me fruitful. The healing was followed by bearing fruit, having success, prosperity, quality of life, and blessing. Only then was Joseph able to fulfill his divine purpose and the vision for his life. God needed Joseph healed in order to use him for His perfect plan.

> **Your Ephraim is supported by your Manasseh. In other words: Your fruits and victories are supported by your healing and deliverance.**

Your pressing on, your advancement throughout your life and moving on to your new time depend on how you relate with your past. Certainly, you can remain hurt, bitter, disappointed and with anger or you can ask God to impregnate you with your Manasseh. You can choose to be a victim all your life and exploit self-pity, blaming your enemies and begging for consolation. You can choose to keep all negative memories alive and live bitter and barren without fruit. You can abort your Ephraim. You can choose to remain imprisoned and shackled or you can say like Paul "forgetting what lies behind I press on to what is ahead."

Future

To proceed you not only have to be free from your past, but you also need to have a point of reference: your future.

You must have a north, a vision. Paul said "extending towards what lies ahead" (future). Paul knew there was more, that he had not walked it all, that he had not exhausted all of what God had for him in this life. Paul was able to see new levels and new times for his life. He knew his life was not only what he had already lived or was living, but that God had planned much more for his life from eternity.

People who lose their vision are brought to a halt. In Hosea 4:6, the prophet declared "My people are destroyed for lack of knowledge." The proverbialist declared, "Where there is no revelation, the people cast off restraint" (Proverbs 29:18). Death, licentiousness, lack of control, deviation, and aimlessness is produced by lack or loss of vision, by not seeing what lies ahead.

> **Only he who has seen what is ahead can say: "I extend and press on."**

"The poorest person in the world is not the person that doesn't have a nickel. The poorest person is the world is the person who doesn't have a vision."[12] The vision (future) always motivates you to move forward, it gives you enthusiasm and provokes in you new strengths. That is why, even if you are in the midst of obstacles, adversity, tiredness and enemies, you will be able to press on because you know that there is more ahead for you. The vision, the prophetic word, the *rhema* word, sustains you in the "pressing on" stage. The word we receive at the beginning of our journey, or even while we are sitting down and kept from advancing, will sustain us in the dark day and will propel us forward.

This has been my personal experience. The vision sustains me in the midst of my walk as a pastor when the difficult times come, when one is alone and the only thing one hears is "it can't be done, it is impossible, this is not of God, the pastor is crazy or he needs therapy." It has sustained me when all I had before me was a mountain, Jericho, or a giant, a Goliath, when I have been in the dark night of my walk. During those times, the vision God has given me is what sustains me. It is that which I have already seen in my spirit, what is ahead for me, that pushes me not to give up and negotiate with the long stretch of valley that I am in and to make the valley my home.

> ## God's vision in my life reminds me that I am on a journey and in transit.

As John Haggai, a great teacher on leadership, says that "what separates the true leaders from others is vision. A vision is important, because it is a key factor in successful leadership."[13]

This is the secret of all of those who press on, of those who want to advance and move to their new time. They have vision. This is why Paul gave this counsel to his son Timothy:

> "This charge I commit to you, son Timothy, according to the prophecies previously made concerning you, that by them you may wage the good warfare."   1st Timothy 1:18

In this text, to wage means to persist, insist, persevere, and not to forget what God has spoken upon you, your calling, and divine purpose. No matter what you are going through or the time it takes, keep the visions alive in your mind and spirit. Speak of them, pray about them, write them, live them, and believe them. That is the same instruction that God gave the Prophet Habakkuk:

> "Write the vision and make it plain on tablets, that he may run who reads it. For the vision is yet for an appointed time; but at the end it will speak, and it will not lie. Though it tarries, wait for it; because it will surely come, it will not tarry."
> Habakkuk 2: 2-3

Writing down your vision is a requirement. You are prohibited from forgetting it even if it takes a long time, it will not delay, it will be fulfilled, but you must press on. Remember that each vision has its time, its "kairos." Each traveler, on his way to his new level, has to bring with him **the written vision**

and he has to run with it. Have you received the vision of God for your life? Are you waging in it? Have you written it on paper and in your spirit or are you letting it die? It is time to extend and press on to what is ahead. Remember: you are a stopover passenger. Press on. Forget your past, take hold of your vision, run with it, and press on.

Chapter 3 Notes

(12) <u>Be all you can be!</u> - John Maxwell - David C. Cook Distribution 2007 (pp. 51-52)
(13) <u>Lead On! Leadership That Endures in a Changing World</u> - John Haggai – Word Publishing 1986 (p. 16)

My Prayer

Lord, I pray that my dear readers may continue forward. Regardless of what they may be going through, I pray they may be able to press on. Help them excuse themselves of any parties that serve only to distract and stop them from the journey to their new level. I pray they may be able to cross the valley and advance to the mountaintop.

Help them conquer the past and keep a firm victory upon them so they can forget everything that is behind and may be able to extend to what is ahead. Revive the vision that you have given them and that each day they may be able to wage in the prophetic word they have received; that they may write down their vision, rise up with it, walk with it, speak of it, pray for it, and lay with it. That they may have the spirit of Paul and say: "Only one thing I do, I press on." In Christ Jesus, we pray. Amen.

My Prophetic Declaration

- I declare it is my time to press on and move forward.

- I declare that what I have begun in the name of Jesus I will finish it.

- I declare it is my time to forget what lies behind and I extend towards what is ahead. I am free of my past, my Manasseh frees my Ephraim.

- I declare I will not remain in the valley, but I will cross it, I will press on towards my goal.

- I declare I will not be entertained and will not waste time in parties when it is my time to be encouraged and move forward.

- I declare I will keep alive the vision God gave me. I wage in it, believe it, speak it, write it, and read it each day. I will run with my vision because it is my point of reference. From it, I receive strength, motivation, and direction to press on.

REST

CHAPTER 4

"He gives power to the weak, and to those who have no might He increases strength... But those who wait on the LORD shall renew their strength; they shall mount up with wings like eagles ..."

Isaiah 40:29, 31

If we want to move to our new season and fulfill God's purpose in our lives, we need to plan certain stops throughout our walk. They are necessary stops, since they are for resting and for the renewing of our being. The reason many people, including leaders and pastors, are stuck in their journeys is not because of fear, laziness, or being conformed. It is simply that they are left without spiritual, emotional, or physical strength. We can summarize the condition and cause in one word: exhaustion.

> **People who are exhausted cannot go anywhere.**
> **To continue you need to rest and renew yourself.**

The mistake many have made is not stopping and resting along the way to regain the strength needed to continue. Each day the number of leaders becoming victims of stress increases because of the excess in work and responsibilities. Many have renounced their vocation, not because God did not call them, but because they are exhausted. They are simply burnt out. They kept on giving non-stop without taking quality time to rest and renew themselves.

It is important to emphasize that when we are fatigued and exhausted, we are prone to make mistakes, to make the wrong decisions, and to lose perspective. Consequently, we are vulnerable to the attacks of the enemy. The relationship between people who are exhausted and the deterioration of physical health, the failure of businesses or enterprises, and the loss of significant relationships is well documented and established.

When people live in continuous stress or tension, they lose their humor and happiness, which affects their immunological system making them prone to illnesses. It is told of a doctor who used to prescribe his hospitalized patients with watching two or three hours of comedy shows. Doing so would help them laugh and disconnect at least to a degree from their stress and problems. His patients improved more than those who had the same condition but did not go under the humor therapy. "A well-developed sense of humor is the pole that adds balance to your steps as you walk the tightrope of life."[14] The proverbialist declared the principle connecting lifestyle and health many centuries before this fabled doctor put it into practice.

> "A merry heart does good, like medicine, but a broken spirit dries the bones."
>
> Proverbs 17:22

Just as laziness is a sin, so is the excess of work. It is sin to deny our being - body, soul, and spirit - a time of rest. There is no contradiction between "continuing" and "resting." By the way, being able to firmly "**continue**" pressing on will depend on the quality and frequency of the "**resting**." To continue forward without resting is risking not finishing the journey and staying half way to your new level, because eventually exhaustion will manifest itself. Rest and renewal are more important than we may believe. Anyone who would like to advance to a new level should, in a rather intentional way, separate quality time frequently to renew himself.

> To deny ourselves rest is to defeat ourselves. It
> opens doors to the enemy and empowers the
> obstacles in our path, making them invincible
> and unconquerable not because they are strong,
> but rather because we are weak.

We live in a culture of continuous production, where producing is valued and encouraged, in such a way that industries, enterprises, and businesses want to produce 24 hours a day, 7 days a week, 12 months a year. This situation turns into a great problem when we as fathers, mothers, spouses, leaders, and pastors also fall into this trend and do not know when to stop.

The Sabbath

God himself gave us the example of the importance of the relationship between rest and work. The creation took six days of work, but on the seventh day, he rested.

> "And on the seventh day God ended His work which
> He had done, and He rested on the seventh day from
> all His work which He had done."
>
> Genesis 2:2

We know that God does not get tired, but he chose to rest after working on the creation to teach us and model how we should live our lives. He not only gave us the example, but also established it as a principle of life when he instituted the Sabbath.

> "Remember the Sabbath day, to keep it holy. Six
> days you shall labor and do all your work, but the
> seventh day is the Sabbath of the LORD your God.
> In it you shall do no work: you, nor your son, nor
> your daughter, nor your male servant, nor your
> female servant, nor your cattle, nor your stranger
> who is within your gates."   Exodus 20:8-10

The Sabbath, as a principle of life, seeks to bring renewal to our being and to creation. I call it a shift in speed, where we let go of worries, duties, preoccupations, and the routine of the workweek to enter into a time of rest and stillness. It is a time for recharging your batteries and regaining your strength. The simple act of changing your schedule and tasks is in itself refreshing and stimulating. Rest is so crucial that in fact the Lord gave an order to his people that every seventh year they should leave the cultivable soil to rest so it can regain its strength and minerals. Part of the objective of the Sabbath was to prolong and improve the quality of life of the Israelites (see Deuteronomy 6:1-3).

> "Now this is the commandment, and these are the statutes and judgments which the LORD your God has commanded to teach you, that you may observe them in the land which you are crossing over to possess, that you may fear the LORD your God, to keep all His statutes and His commandments which I command you, you and your son and your grandson, all the days of your life, and **that your days may be prolonged**. Therefore, hear, O Israel, and be careful to observe it, **that it may be well with you** ..."

When you live according to divine precepts, the result will be to prolong and improve your quality of life.

For me, the Sunday service experience is renewing, capturing the spirit and essence of the Sabbath. It is a service with a therapeutic dimension that we should not miss, for it gives us new strength to continue pressing on during the rest of the week. Psalm 149:1-4 describes it in a very assertive way.

> "Praise the LORD! Sing to the LORD a new song, and His praise in the assembly of saints. Let Israel rejoice in their Maker; let the children of Zion be joyful in their King. Let them praise His name with the dance; Let them sing praises to Him with the timbrel and harp. For the LORD takes pleasure in His people; he will beautify the humble with salvation."

Sunday is the day where all the saints gather to sing to the Lord, to rejoice in our Creator, to rejoice in our King, and we do it with songs, dance, and with instruments. It is a spiritual party where God himself is present and rejoices along with his people. As a result, God embellishes us with His salvation: that is with life, blessings, health, and with His Shalom. When we flow in an attitude of praise and worship, participate in a time of prayer and intercession, and at the same time, we receive a powerful Word, the result is that we are integrally renewed and we leave the event or experience with new strength, faith, and energy to face our daily life and common struggles.

People who do not attend Sunday services miss these benefits and instead continue to accumulate new burdens with their old ones during the week. Consequently, it should not be a surprise when they have a terrible week and lose their enthusiasm in life. It is sad to see how some people come to the service and waste away such precious time in the presence of God. Instead of doing what Psalm 149 says, they spend their time talking, walking around the church, sleeping or choosing to be spectators instead of participating in the experience and in so doing being renewed. They were in the service, but left the same way they came. It is like going to a restaurant, paying for the food, and leaving the place without eating.

Psalm 23

The shepherd of Psalm 23 knew the balance between continuing forth and resting. The shepherd knows that one of his responsibilities is to lead the flock on the right path. But he also knows that it is his responsibility to take them to still waters and green pastures so they can rest.

> "He makes me to lie down in green pastures; he leads me beside the still waters."
>
> Psalm 23:2

> "He leads me in the paths of righteousness for His name's sake."   Psalm 23:3b

A good shepherd works to establish this balance. He knows both approaches well; he knows when it is time to advance and when it is time to go to the still waters. When the shepherd takes his flock to the green pastures, he knows it is time to rest and does not see it as a waste of time, but rather as a good investment.

Many of us, rather than enjoy it, feel guilty when the time of green pastures and still waters (i.e., our time to rest or take a vacation) arrives. This is especially true of leaders and pastors. The reason for this is that we think we are wasting time and should be working, because we do not feel we are tired. In reality, we are responding to a secular philosophy.

Our mind gravitates to work and even though we are in the "still waters," emotionally and mentally we are behind the desk, the business or the pulpit when we should be resting. The problem for many of us is that we do not know how to disconnect ourselves from work and concentrate on resting. The result is we return to work and to our duties without renewing ourselves, just as tired and with the same level of stress.

It is important not to confuse work with busyness. Busyness, for me is to be continually in movement, doing something, producing something, for the sake of not being still. It is to do things, even though it may not be my job to do them, nor coincide with the purpose of God for my life. There is a time to be active, and there is a time to be still.

One of the social problems that are rarely spoken about is work addiction. Because you want to be working all the time, you deny time for your family, your children, and your spouse. You deny time for yourself to rest and do some other good things, like spending time with your friends, playing a sport, sleeping, going on vacations, going to church events or spending intimate time with God. If this is your case, seek help, because it is possible that you are addicted to work or to money.

My experience

For a long time, my day of rest as a pastor has been Monday. It is the only day of the week that we do not have activities in church during the day or at night. It is the day my wife and I can do other things and concentrate on one another. Nevertheless, even though I understood this principle and separated a time for rest, I used to boycott the time and use this day for any unforeseen meetings or needs of the church. If anyone needed a counseling session and there was no other day available, I would use Mondays and continue doing the same thing repeatedly. My wife confronted me with this reality and asked me if it was truly our day off because it was not working for us. From that moment on, I have respected our day of rest.

Even after resolving to take this day to be with each other, I had to overcome another obstacle. Though I was with her all day, my mind was still at work. My wife was spending the day with a sleepwalker. I still had not learned to disconnect myself from work so I could concentrate on my day off. I was not enjoying other things, or benefiting from a time of being renewed when you stop doing what you normally do. Again, my wife talked to me about this issue and I had to accept that it was true. I had to start putting my best effort forward in order to maximize my time of rest and renewal. I believe that many pastors' wives understand what I am talking about. Even though it was not easy for me, I want to say that it can be done. This time has been so beneficial for the both us that now I am the one who defends it and looks forward to it.

Sometimes we want to appear to be more spiritual than God and Jesus himself. Let us look at Jesus in His ministry while He was here on Earth. He never wasted His time, but rather knew and understood His mission (see Luke 4:18-19). He did not want any distractions because He knew that His time was limited.

> "I must work the works of Him who sent Me while it is day; the night is coming when no one can work."
>
> John 9:4

Nevertheless, we see that after some time He would separate himself from the multitude needing to go to a separate place to rest (Matthew 14:13). We see Him in Mark 4:38 sleeping on the boat with His disciples when they were surprised and overcome by a storm (He used the time to take a nap). We see Him frequently going to the house of His friend Lazarus and His sisters Mary and Martha. There Jesus could rest and eat well (Luke 10:38). Resting was part of Jesus' message to the people and that is why He practiced it.

> "Come to Me, all you who labor and are heavy laden,
> and I will give you rest."   Matthew 11:28

It is important we learn to take vacations every so often during the year. Vacations should be planned and budgeted for as part of our action plan and strategy to fulfill our goals. Vacations should not be in conflict with our "pressing on." Vacations should be a motive for prayer like any other petition or need. I am still growing this area, because if it were up to me, I would never take them. This is the reason why you cannot leave vacations for whenever it becomes possible. We have to be intentional about it. All churches should make sure their pastors along with their families take vacations on a regular basis, and bless them financially so they do not have to limit themselves to places of low category.

Mary and Martha

Let us evaluate the example of Mary and Martha, Lazarus' sisters, a family that had befriended Jesus. The great difference between these two sisters was that Mary was able to recognize her time of rest and Martha did not. Mary knew how to put the tasks and the demands of the day aside to sit at Jesus' feet, while Martha continued working without stopping. Jesus clearly diagnosed Martha's condition:

> "Martha, Martha, you are worried and troubled
> about many things."   Luke 10:41

Jesus tells her that she is anxious, stressed, disturbed, since she could not discern that Jesus had come so they could enjoy a time of still waters. Furthermore, she was upset with Mary for sitting down and leaving the chores aside and with Jesus for interrupting their cleaning. Notice Martha tried to create guilt in Mary for taking the time to renew herself. Martha referred to Mary as if she was lazy and irresponsible.

From Martha's perspective, Mary was wrong, but from Jesus' perspective, Martha was wrong. You have to be careful with those people who want to kill themselves working and want others to do the same. I believe Martha's condition may be the condition of many nowadays. We are in such a rush that we do not know how to stop, be still, and take time to "sit at the feet of Jesus" and worship him. There are many ministries styled after Martha, but few are like Mary. A lot of movement and over activity, but little worship and rest before the Lord.

Esau's case

In Esau's story, we have a clear example of this message. There is great danger in making decisions when you are exhausted. Why was it so easy for Jacob to convince Esau to exchange his blessing for some stew? It was easy because Esau was completely exhausted after a long day of hunting.

> "Now Jacob cooked a stew; and Esau came in from the field, and he was weary. And Esau said to Jacob, 'Please feed me with that same red stew, for I am weary.' Therefore his name was called Edom. But Jacob said, 'Sell me your birthright as of this day.' And Esau said, 'Look, I am about to die; so what is this birthright to me?'"   Genesis 25:29-32

People who are weak and exhausted tend to make bad decisions.

Throughout that day, Esau did not take time to rest and take in some nourishment. He overlooked the time of resting and eating. That is why he was vulnerable to Jacob's offer. I am almost convinced the story would have been different, if when Jacob arrived with his food he found Esau rested and without hunger. Tiredness and hunger did not allow him to think well, but instead, made him lose his perspective and make a bad decision, a decision that followed him every day of his life. This is not a game; knowing how to rest can affect the rest of our life.

> "Lest there be any fornicator or profane person like Esau, who for one morsel of food sold his birthright. For you know that afterward, when he wanted to inherit the blessing, he was rejected, for he found no place for repentance, though he sought it diligently with tears." Hebrews 12:16-17

The case of the Prophet Elijah

Consider Prophet Elijah's case. After total success against the prophets of Baal and Asherah on Mount Carmel, we find him running away desperately at the threat he received from the wicked queen Jezebel. Now we see an Elijah who is suffering what psychologist today call stress syndrome or vocational burnout. To have some understanding of the way the prophet reacted we need to see the amount of hard and intense work he faced (1st Kings 18:30-40).

Elijah confronted the prophets of Baal and every spiritual confrontation drains one's strength. Then he took the task of prepairing the altar by carrying stones and edifying the altar to the Lord. Then he dug a trench around it, arranged the wood, cut the bull into pieces, and laid the bull offering on the wood. Finally, he beheaded the 450 prophets of Baal. All this demanded a great investment of physical and emotional energy. These prolonged and intense events were done by the prophet without any sort of help.

It should not be a surprise when the next confrontation comes, this time on behalf of Jezebel who promises to kill him the same way he killed her prophets, Elijah runs away. When we find him in hiding, he has been under pressure and overworked for quite a while with no time to rest or renew his strength. It should not be surprising then that he decides to run away. The prophet, who successfully faced the prophets of Baal, turns into a stressed and exhausted prophet.

> "And when he saw that, he arose and ran for his life, and went to Beersheba, which belongs to Judah, and left his servant there. But he himself went a day's journey into the wilderness, and came and sat down under a broom tree. And he prayed that he might die, and said, 'It is enough! Now, LORD, take my life, for I am no better than my fathers!' Then as he lay and slept under a broom tree, suddenly an angel touched him, and said to him, 'Arise and eat.'"
>
> 1st Kings 19:3-5

> "So he arose, and ate and drank; and he went in the strength of that food forty days and forty nights as far as Horeb, the mountain of God. And there he went into a cave, and spent the night in that place ..."
>
> 1st Kings 19:8-9

Elijah exhibits many of the characteristics of people who face vocational burnout:

- **Escapism**
  Abandons the city where the problem is, the crisis, thinking that, because he is running away, the problems will be solved.

- **Isolation**
  Stops contact with every person and place, and does not want to be with or talk with anyone. That is why he goes to the desert and hides in a cave.

- **Depression**
  We see him sad and afflicted even in the way he prays and in choosing to hide in a dark and humid cave. Escapism and isolation are characteristic of a person who is depressed.

- **Assuming the role of victim**
  Believes that he is the only one who suffers, that no one understands or comprehends him, not even God, that what he is going through is unjust. Exploits pity.

- **Resignation and defeat**
  Given everything that is happening, why even bother continuing forward? It is better to die and for everything to end. He has internalized the spirit of defeat.

It is important to notice the terrible consequences that not resting and not renewing can bring to our lives. If you are in this situation or nearing it, it is important to pay attention to what may happen.

The passage says God goes in search of the prophet to restore and minister to him. It is interesting the way the Lord ministers to him, because it is tailored to the situation the prophet is going through. The Lord knows all the fear, desperation, anguish, depression, sadness, and the anxiety the prophet is experiencing. The Lord knows the prophet has not slept in days, nor eaten, and that is why he lets him sleep. Then he sends the angel with food.

> "Then as he lay and slept under a broom tree, suddenly an angel touched him, and said to him, 'Arise and eat.' Then he looked, and there by his head was a cake baked on coals, and a jar of water. So he ate and drank, and lay down again."
> 1st Kings 19:5-6

Elijah needed not only a spiritual ministration, but also a physical one. He needed both things. Observe how linked the physical dimension is to the spiritual. To neglect the physical in the long run, will affect the spiritual and vice versa. We cannot continue to operate in a manner that separates the spirit and the body as if they were two different entities. We are a single being. In the following verses, the prophet eats again, is strengthened, and is able to walk fasting for forty days. Can you see the relation between taking care of the physical dimension and the direct result in the spiritual?

> "And the angel of the LORD came back the second time, and touched him, and said, 'Arise and eat, because the journey is too great for you.' So he arose, and ate and drank; and he went in the strength of that food forty days and forty nights as far as Horeb, the mountain of God." 1st Kings 19:7-8

It is later in the cave that the Lord orders him to come out and go up to the mountain of God, to the high place and stand right before him, right before his presence. The prophet then experiences a great wind, a strong earthquake and then an intense fire, but the Lord was not in any of those manifestations. Finally, a gentle whisper comes and it is there where God is found and where Elijah is ministered to (see 1st Kings 19:9-18). Elijah was ministered through the peace that comes from God. When the Lord visits him, his being was refreshed, renewed, and he received rest and new strength.

David

King David knew about the secret of renewal. He knew that in the presence of the Lord there is fullness of joy and eternal pleasures at his right hand. He knew that under his wings (his arms) he could rejoice. He knew the Lord is the one who lifted up his head. David knew the gentle whisper that turned into new strength, joy, enthusiasm, and life.

> "You will show me the path of life; in Your presence is fullness of joy; at Your right hand are pleasures forevermore." Psalm 16:11

> "Because You have been my help, therefore in the shadow of Your wings I will rejoice." Psalm 63:7

> "But You, O LORD, are a shield for me, my glory and the One who lifts up my head." Psalm 3:3

- What a difference between a person who is exhausted and depressed and the one who is rested and renewed!

• What a difference between a person who is hidden in a cave and the one standing in front of God in His high place!

• What a difference between a person who is burdened with stress and the one who has been ministered by the gentle whisper of the Lord!

> **All of us are in danger of acting like Elijah believing that everything has ended. But it is good for you to know the Lord who restored Elijah, is still active and calling those who are in caves to meet Him in the high place.**

When Elijah thought everything had ended for him in such a negative way, God ministered to him and told him the following:

> "Then the LORD said to him: 'Go, return on your way to the Wilderness of Damascus; and when you arrive, anoint Hazael as king over Syria. Also you shall anoint Jehu the son of Nimshi as king over Israel. And Elisha the son of Shaphat of Abel Meholah you shall anoint as prophet in your place.'"
>
> 1st Kings 19:15-16

God made him return to his mission and his place of ministry so that he could finish in a powerful and successful way, giving him new instructions: to anoint kings and anoint his successor as a prophet.

Pay attention to how Elijah wanted to finish his ministry: under a tree in the desert, running away from Jezebel. All this happens to him due to his exhaustion. Nevertheless, we see God had another plan, a better one. Instead of dying under the hand of Jezebel, God sends him to prophesy her death and even the way in which Jezebel was to die (1st Kings 21:23). The plan of God was not for Elijah to die under a tree; God's plan was to send for him in a chariot of fire, escaping the

grips of death altogether. Elijah almost lost this privilege, one
that has only been given to Enoch and Christ.

> "Then it happened, as they continued on and talked,
> that suddenly a chariot of fire appeared with horses
> of fire, and separated the two of them; and Elijah
> went up by a whirlwind into heaven."
>
> 2nd Kings 2:11

**We definitely need to give thanks to God for the
times he chooses not to answer our prayers,
because what we have asked for is not in
agreement with God's perfect plan for us.**

Elijah prayed for God to take his life away under that
tree, but God's plan was much better. Internalize and take note
of what a state of constant tiredness and exhaustion can do to a
person.

Renewed like eagles

The Prophet Isaiah also discovered the secret of renewal
for all those who want to press on in their walk of faith. He
declares that the Lord multiplies the strength of those who
have no might, and gives strength to the weary. He goes on to
say those who wait upon the Lord will soar on wings like
eagles. God gives revelation to the prophet about his renewing
power and provision of new strength symbolically using the
image of an eagle.

> "He gives power to the weak, and to those who have
> no might He increases strength. But those who wait
> on the LORD shall renew their strength; they shall
> mount up with wings like eagles, they shall run and
> not be weary, they shall walk and not faint."
>
> Isaiah 40: 29, 31

The will of God is that we may be renewed in the same
way that an eagle renews itself, so we can continue on our race
until we finish. When the eagle is aging it goes to a hidden and

private place, and it is there the process of renewing begins. The eagle separates this time, it is on the calendar, and there the bird awaits the onset of its new feathers, beak, and claws.

> **There is no other way for the eagle to renew itself but to be still. Renewal always demands a time to wait upon the Lord.**

It is said that if the eagle does not take off its old feathers, the new feathers will come in regardless and it will not be able to fly due to excess weight, and it will consequently die. At the same time if the old and bent beak is not removed, then the new one will not come in as it should, and the eagle will die of hunger since with a bent beak it is impossible for it to eat.

The message of the eagle is clear: if it does not renew itself, it dies. Even if renewal implies pain, it is a necessary pain. You need to understand that renewing implies a degree of waiting, loss, and pain. Renewing entails a price. Remember, if we do not learn how to renew ourselves, rest and receive new strength, we will die. The dead cannot continue and finish their race.

You can choose to be like an eagle. Separate your time for renewing yourself and let go of your old feathers. You can choose to be like Elijah; come out of the cave and stand in the high place right before Jehovah. Renew and press on.

Chapter 4 Notes

(14) <u>You can reach the top</u> - Zig Ziglar - Cook Communications Ministries 2005 (p. 194)

My Prayer

Lord, I ask you help my readers understand the importance of resting and renewing their being, as a vital part of their pressing on. That they can, in an intentional way, separate a formal time to recover their physical, emotional, and spiritual strengths. That they can understand that their pressing on to their new season is connected with their rest stops along the way.

Help them enjoy the still waters and green pastures that you have for them throughout their journey. Guard them from all over activity and excess work. In the same manner, break any addictions to work or money if it is necessary.

I ask you that they may always make the best decisions because their minds are rested and their spirits are alert, so their advancement is not affected by the quality of their decisions. That each Sunday they can make a stop to go to the worship service, preaching and prayer, and while they worship and thank you, that you would minister to them as you did to Elijah in the high place.

That they are able to renew themselves like the eagle and let go of any old feathers, so in the end they can return with renewed strength, enthusiasm, and determination to their journey, to their new season. In Christ Jesus, we pray. Amen.

My Prophetic Declaration

- I declare I will stop for rest and renewal each time it is necessary in order to be renewed and strengthened always.

- I declare I am free of any over activity and work addiction and I will know to enjoy my green pastures and still waters.

- I declare I belong to the heights of God and not to the caves of depression. That I will not die under a tree, for a long journey still remains. I rebuke every depression, defeat and any spirit that would lead me to make myself a victim.

- I declare that each Sunday I will go to the service of my local church, because it is a time where I can be intimate with God and be renewed by Him.

- I declare that like the eagle I will intentionally separate time to recover new strength and that I will let go of any old feathers. That I will not die, but I will soar on wings and advance to my new season.

- I declare I am strong, renewed, rested, and filled with energy to continue towards my new level.

OBSTACLES

CHAPTER 5

"For assuredly, I say to you, whoever says to this mountain, 'Be removed and be cast into the sea,' and does not doubt in his heart, but believes that those things he says will be done, he will have whatever he says." Mark 11:23

In order to move forward to your new season you need to learn how to overcome obstacles. It is impossible to move forward to your new season without finding obstacles, resistance, and opposition along the way. I wish I could tell you the road towards your next level or season is expedient and free of obstacles, but the reality is the road will at times be a rocky one. In many occasions, it will be a dark road, with many crossroads, mountains and giants, filled with uncertainty, where every decision has an impact on your ability to progress forward.

> **Being able to continue will depend on your capacity to conquer and overcome the obstacles.**

In order to overcome the obstacles in our way, we need to re-examine our way of viewing them. Why do I say this? Because we have always viewed obstacles as something negative that comes to take us out of our path. But if we face obstacles correctly, they will become themselves a positive force that will push us to our new level. Let me share with you four ways of viewing obstacles in a different manner.

1) The obstacles are a confirmation of your goals.

Remember that without Goliath, David would have never reached his promotion from the field to the palace, from a pastor of sheep to becoming the right hand and captain of Saul's army. Joseph told his brothers that everything they had planned for evil, in the end it turned out for the good, because God changed him. Ultimately, selling Joseph as a slave who was then taken to Egypt facilitated the very vision his brothers were opposing. It came to pass in great part through their very actions. Interesting!

Identifying an obstacle is the confirmation of having a goal. By definition, an obstacle is whatever is between you and your objective, something that gets in the way between you and what you desire. Only the people who have goals have obstacles. If you have obstacles right this instant, that means you have goals, you are fighting to get those things you still do not have and would like to reach, and you want to be places you have never been. Your obstacles are a confirmation you are a person with goals. I congratulate you, not for your obstacles, but for being a person with aspirations and goals.

> **Having obstacles is not really a problem. To lack them is the real problem, because of what it says about you: that you do not have aspirations, dreams, or visions.**

To live a life without facing obstacles means that you are detained, sitting, vegetating, and about to die. If you are going north, a mountain in the south is not an obstacle for you. But if that mountain were north and in your path, then it turns into an obstacle the moment your goal takes you north through the mountain. Your goals define the obstacles in your life.

> **Your goals define the obstacles.**

There are people, who instead of confronting their obstacle, give up on their goal. The way of overcoming "your mountain" is not by giving up your goal, but rather conquering it by climbing over it, going through it, or blasting it away. Zig Ziglar says the following regarding this subject: "When obstacles arise, change your direction to reach your goal; not the decision to get there."[15]

2) The obstacles testify the type of person you are.

When you have goals, and obviously I am referring to positive goals and objectives, approved by God, that are in agreement with the calling and purpose of God in your life, that makes you a special person and it distinguishes you from many other people. A great number of people lack goals, longings, desires, dreams, and visions. They do not live, but rather only exist. Your obstacles are the confirmation you are not just one more from the crowd, but you are different. My advice to you is not to focus on obstacles and opposition as the main issue when they come. Focus on your goals. Do not ever lose sight of the reason why that mountain or giant is an obstacle for you.

The purpose of the obstacle is to block your way, to confine you to the place you have always been. It is there to get you from making progress and get you to abandon your goals. Many people pity those who are fighting against obstacles and say "poor him, looks like he is struggling." But I interpret it in a different manner. I do not feel pity for them, but on the contrary, they are a motivation for me. A person who faces obstacles sends me the message that they have no plans of making pacts with mediocrity and that they do not have a conformed spirit. The message they send me is that they are tired of being in the same place, doing and having the same things, while knowing there is more; they will not abandon their goals. Do not feel sadness or pity for yourself. Do not live like a victim just because you are facing opposition. Take heart, because you have left your comfort zone to set loose a new season for your life.

I consider myself a visionary and without a doubt, every visionary will face opposition. Every story about a visionary needs to dedicate some time to address the obstacles.

It is not possible to speak about Joshua without speaking about Jericho or to speak about David without mentioning Goliath. When we think of Nehemiah, we think about Sanballat. We also associate Moses with the Pharaoh, and Deborah with Sisera. In other words, it is impossible to talk about victories or new seasons without talking about obstacles and adversities.

Many people congratulate me for the ministry the Lord has given us in the city of Springfield. They come and see the accomplishments, blessings, provisions, and harvest. They rejoice with us. What they do not know is that behind each one of those blessings is a story of obstacles and oppositions. When my family and I arrived to the city of Springfield as pastors, the leadership running the church presented us with a financial offer, and it was good. In that same breath they went on to say that there was a small problem: they did not have the money in hand to make it a reality. That is how our ministry in Springfield began.

We arrived to a new and unfamiliar city from Puerto Rico, without friends, without being able to speak the language. We came from a tropical climate to a place in the United States where some of the worst winters take place. To top it all off, we had to face racial prejudice, especially for our children. In Puerto Rico, we had our own house and in Springfield, we had to rent various houses each with many serious limitations. In the island, we had a comfortable car, which we ended up selling with the move, and it was that sale that helped us financially during the first few months, since the church was only able to give us some small contributions. The first car we had in Springfield was about ten years old and did not meet the basic needs of my family.

As far as the church, it only had 19 members and an attendance of between 30 and 40 people, including children and visitors. The first thing some of the church members told me was that as soon the summer came they would move to Puerto Rico because they could not bear another winter season. The church did not have its own temple, but was renting a small chapel from an African-American Baptist Church. The church did not have heat and it was so cold during the services people would not take their coats off for fear of getting sick. We also did not have any ventilation and in the summer the heat was so unbearable we were almost in danger of having people faint during the service. We did not have an office, phones, or enough parking spaces. The church did not even have a promotional sign with its name on it.

In Puerto Rico, several of my friends who are pastors told me: do not go to that region, that place is spiritually arid. None of our churches have grown there and all of our pastors who have gone there return in less than 5 years without accomplishing much.

When I speak about facing obstacles, you can believe me that I know what I am talking about. My experience has been that every time the Lord wants to promote us to a new time, level or season, together with a new vision, the prophetic word (rhema) is accompanied with opposition. It is an opposition that comes to impede you from moving to that new level and confine you to the place you have always been.

I give the Glory to God, because each obstacle was overcome. At this time our church is experiencing growth in numbers and spiritually. The church is one of the biggest in the city and in the Pioneer Valley. We acquired a temple for six-hundred thousand dollars some years ago with spacious facilities and parking spaces, which are now completely paid off along with a two level house right next to the temple, which is also paid off. Not too long ago we purchased another building in the city of Holyoke to establish another Apostolic Renewal Church.

We have different ministries for the community like the food pantry ministry (Open Pantry), TV and Internet ministries, recordings, bookstore, children's ministry, youth, single women, and marriages. We have our Leadership Academy, evangelism ministry, intercession, and the ministry of Renewal Family Groups (small groups that meet weekly in the homes of our members). We have 18 pastors, full-time staff and others who work part-time. We have a ministry for the nations (International Apostolic Renewal Network) where we have established churches in different countries like Perú,

Argentina, Dominican Republic, Honduras, and Puerto Rico. We are also associated with other churches in different nations and are providing spiritual covering to more than 40 pastors. The brothers and sisters from the local church are the ones who, with their prayers, courage, and financial support sustain both the local vision and the vision for the nations. We have seen that where it was once thought nothing could be done, that indeed it can but we had to face obstacles. Learn this: do not wait for the easy way or an unobstructed path to open up. The land that you are going to possess is filled with enemies that you have to deal with and get rid of. God told Joshua to cross over the Jordan and step on the land, but He also told him that he had to expel the enemies; he had to surround and conquer Jericho, a city surrounded by walls.

3) **The obstacles have the potential of releasing the best in you.**

Many of us do not know how much we are able to do until we have to face obstacles and crisis. We fail to know all the abilities, gifts, and capacities that God has placed inside of us. The full potential we have within can truly manifest itself and we can get to know ourselves much more intricately when we face obstacles, adversities, and opposition. We will not know what we are able to do and what we are capable of until we are face-to-face with the obstacles and opposition.

It has been scientifically proven that when a person is under a lot of tension or in danger, they can do things that normally could not be done. It releases in us that substance called adrenaline that gives us the energy, power, and courage to do things that are "out of this world" and extraordinary. Some time ago, we heard the news of a woman and her son who suffered a terrible car accident where the car had turned over. She was able to get out but her son was trapped in the back seat. The car caught on fire and started bursting out flames and in her desperation; she lifted up part of the car and was able to take her son out and into safety. Under normal circumstances, she would have never been able to lift up that car, not even a tiny bit. She was a small woman and did not weigh much, but the crisis released a strength in her that enabled her to overcome that obstacle.[16]

I have seen people in great poverty ... overcome; chronically sick people ... overcome; people who have suffered failure after failure ... overcome. The same thing that was holding them back or stopping them was the source of motivation to overcome. Perhaps without those obstacles, many people would not have reached as high a level in their lives.

If throughout our lives we live in controlled and peaceful environments where nothing happens, we will never grow, develop to the maximum, or release our promotion. Challenges and obstacles have their place in life. They are needed to prevent us from becoming weak, soft, and scrawny or without character. I like the way Helen Keller, a blind person who overcame throughout her life, said it:

> "Character cannot be developed in ease and quiet. Only through experience of trial and suffering can the soul be strengthened, ambition inspired, and success achieved." [17]

Your most critical moment could turn into your best moment.

To go a bit further, there are people who when they see you in front of your mountain or giant, will call the funeral home and will offer to apply over you an extreme unction or last rites believing you will die. Nevertheless, they do not know that from the same crisis and opposition, new strength will be born and capacities that have yet to manifest themselves will surface. From those experiences of opposition, you will be more mature, wiser, calmer, and more eager to continue forward, to press on.

There are things we can already do, but we will not know we can do them until we face obstacles.

---

4) Obstacles are opportunities for God to show off.

Obstacles not only have the potential to bring out the best that God has placed in us, but they are also a time for God to show that He is God. It is the time in which God will be glorified. All the miracles that are registered in the Bible and all the wonders took place in times of crisis and adversity. Therefore, if you are in the midst of some difficult times, you qualify for your miracle. God shows his power in the crisis, in our limitations.

Remember that Paul discovered that when he was weak then he was strong, because God's power is made perfect in his weakness.

> "My grace is sufficient for you, for My strength is made perfect in weakness."
>
> 2nd Corinthians 12:9

It is in this context, while many see it as impossible or difficult, where miracles flourish. These situations are the ones that prepare the stage for God to show his power.

Sarah laughed when she heard God tell Abraham that they will both bear a son, because for Sarah the obstacle of being barren was impossible to conquer. Read what the Word of God says that the Lord said to Abraham:

> "Why did Sarah laugh, saying, 'Shall I surely bear a child, since I am old?' Is anything too hard for the LORD? At the appointed time I will return to you, according to the time of life, and Sarah shall have a son." Genesis 18:13-14

Moses told the Lord he could not be the servant to free the Israelites from the hand of Pharaoh because of who he was. He did not have any authority and besides he was slow of speech, but look at what the Lord told him in Exodus 3:12, 15 and 4:11-12.

> "I will certainly be with you ..."
> "Thus you shall say to the children of Israel: 'The LORD God of your fathers, the God of Abraham, the

God of Isaac, and the God of Jacob, has sent me to you. This is My name forever ...'"
"Who has made man's mouth? ... Now therefore, go, and I will be with your mouth and teach you what you shall say."

Jairus' friends told him not to bother Jesus because his daughter had already died; nothing could be done. But Jesus said to Jairus:

> "Do not be afraid; only believe."   Mark 5:36

Martha told Jesus he had arrived at her house late, since it had been four days that Lazarus died. However, look at what Jesus told her:

> "I am the resurrection and the life. He who believes in Me, though he may die, he shall live."
> John 11:25

Remember it was during the time of drought, the most difficult time, that the ravens and the widow of Zarephath miraculously fed Prophet Elijah.

One of the reasons why the Lord brought the people of Israel to the desert was to make them understand and to show them that everything they needed was God himself. Who would think of bringing such numerous people, with children, and elders through the desert? In a place where there is no water or food, in a place where it is intensively hot during the day and cold at the night. Who would think of something like this? So many obstacles! Again there, where it seemed impossible, God glorified himself. I like it the way Psalm 105:37, 39-41 expresses it.

> "He also brought them out with silver and gold, and there was none feeble among His tribes. He spread a cloud for a covering, and fire to give light in the night. The people asked, and He brought quail, and satisfied them with the bread of heaven. He opened the rock, and water gushed out; it ran in the dry places like a river."

I tell you again if you are in the midst of difficult times, of a crisis, or a problem, all of these prior examples testify that you qualify for your miracle.

I would like to share with you some more advice that will help you at the time you face the obstacles that impede you from moving to your new level. In the decisive moment, do not forget them.

More advice

A) To overcome your obstacles you will have to wage spiritual warfare.

If you want to advance to your new season, you will have to turn into a spiritual warrior and wage war, whether you like it or not. It is not possible to overcome opposition without facing it adequately. You have to wage spiritual warfare, because you will face enemies along the road on your way to your new time. Paul was able to finish his race and keep his faith because he knew how to fight the good fight (2nd Timothy 4:7). He gave that same advice to Timothy, his spiritual son.

> "You therefore must endure hardship as a good soldier of Jesus Christ." 2nd Timothy 2:3

David was not only a great musician, attractive, prudent, and wise. He was also brave, a man of war and knew Jehovah was with him (2nd Samuel 16:18).

You not only have to wage war against your problem or mountain, but the war is against anything that opposes the plans of God for your life.

> Not everyone is happy and agrees with your plans to take you to a new season or level. Not everyone will support you in your vision.

Not everyone is happy and agrees with your plans to take you to a new season. Not everyone will support you in your vision. In fact, some people believe it is their ministry and purpose in life to oppose you and your vision. That is why they will make your life difficult. Look again at the case of Joseph's brothers. They were not happy with the visions or the dreams God gave Joseph. Instead, they were jealous, could not stand Joseph, and even wanted to kill him.

> "Look, this dreamer is coming! Come therefore, let
> us now kill him and cast him into some pit …"
>
> Genesis 37:19-20

That spirit and attitude continues to persist in many people today. There still exists a lineage of Joseph's brothers who rise up against the visionaries of this age (visionary killers). We cannot deny that reality and have to be ready to face such opposition in a wise and spiritual manner. Above all, we have a spiritual enemy, the real enemy. He is looking to devour us. The Bible says he is not improvising with respect to you but instead seeks your destruction.

The words trap, schemes, and machinations that are used to describe the work of the enemy against us, implies his attacks are well planned, scheduled, purposeful, and strategically selected to destroy us. This is why Paul advices us not to ignore the schemes of the enemy, in order that Satan might not outwit us (2nd Corinthians 2:11).

As a soldier of Jesus Christ, I need to have character, discipline, training, and understand the spiritual weapons of God available to me that have divine power to demolish strongholds (2nd Corinthians 10:4). In other words, we have to wage war wisely with the enemy or opposition. To overcome opposition we need to have prayer and vigils, days of fasting with prayer, of spiritual warfare and prophetic intercession. We have to take a moment to face the mountain and speak to it the way Jesus did in Mark 11:23.

Sometimes what is needed is to order the mountain to move aside. That is spiritual warfare since we are not speaking about just any mountain but the very mountain that opposes the plans of God and seeks to prevent us from doing that which He chose us to do from before the foundations of the world.

The will be moments that:

- Like David we have to take hold of our own "sling shot and five stones," and go out to face our Goliath; speak to our Goliath the way David spoke and destroy him.

- Like Joshua we have to surround our Jericho, play the *shofar,* and give a shout of war until the walls come trembling down.

- Like Moses we have to raise our staff forward and order the Red Sea to split in half and open up for us to cross and walk on dry land.

All these stories of confrontations taught to us since we were children in bible school are examples of spiritual warfare. Without fighting these battles, the obstacles faced by the different protagonists would not have been conquered.

B) To overcome obstacles you need to learn to encourage yourself.

We have already said a person who is discouraged, tired, and without faith will not go forward. When facing obstacles and opposition we should maintain a good spirit and enthusiasm. We know that along the way God will send people to help us and above all, to encourage us to continue forward. Nevertheless, I have learned during my pastoral walk that I have to be part of that group who encourages themselves. The first cheerleader in your life has to be yourself. You have to be your best friend and the one who most believes in what you are doing. It has to be that way because there will be some difficult times along the way where the only ones there will be you and your mountain, you and your crisis, you and your adversity. It is there where you have to encourage yourself and you cannot run the risk of staying silent.

You have to learn to talk to yourself, correct yourself, and give yourself encouragement. David would speak to himself continuously.

> "Bless the LORD, O my soul, and forget not all His benefits."   Psalm 103:2

In Psalm 42:5, he would correct his soul and say:

> "Why are you cast down, O my soul? And why are you disquieted within me? Hope in God, for I shall yet praise Him for the help of His countenance."

The prodigal son also talked to himself.

> "How many of my father's hired servants have bread enough and to spare, and I perish with hunger! I will arise and go to my father ..."   Luke 15:17-18

To talk, encourage, and correct yourself appropriately you have to do it according to the Word of God. The Bible tells us that our thoughts need to be based on positive things. In other words, if you are going to think, think right.

> "Finally, brethren, whatever things are true, whatever things are noble, whatever things are just, whatever things are pure, whatever things are lovely, whatever things are of good report, if there is any virtue and if there is anything praiseworthy – meditate on these things."   Philippians 4:8

The Word makes us confess and speak positively. The Prophet Joel ordered the people to say:

> "Let the weak say, 'I am strong.'"   Joel 3:10

Similarly, the Apostle Paul taught that we should proclaim victory even in the midst of adversity:

> "Who shall separate us from the love of Christ? Shall tribulation, or distress, or persecution, or famine, or nakedness, or peril, or sword? **Yet in all these things we are more than conquerors through Him who loved us.**"   Romans 8:35, 37

> Instead of counting the reasons why you can fail, enumerate the reasons why you can overcome.

What you think and speak over your life is a key factor to overcome your obstacles and enemies. If you do not trust yourself to go forward and encourage yourself to press on, how can you expect other people to trust you? You cannot make anyone else believe in your dreams and visions, but you can at least convince yourself.

C) To overcome obstacles you need to be persistent.

When we speak of overcoming obstacles we have to make mention of persistence, since it needs to be an integral part of the profile of those who would like to advance to their new season. Persistence is an indispensable ingredient at the time of conquering obstacles, because to overcome them is not a task that is easily brushed aside or completed in few minutes. It is imperative that we develop a persistent and unrelenting spirit. We need the spirit of Jacob, who spent a whole night fighting with an angel telling him: "I will not let go of you until you bless me." Persistence is the way of life of those who if they cannot cross a mountain, they will blow right through it, or will give the mountain the order to move aside. Perhaps they might even purchase the mountain, level it, or use it to fill in other areas. They might even get a helicopter and go over it, but they will continue trying until they overcome it.

What type of person are you? Do you give up the first time you are criticized? Do you get discouraged in the first round of fighting or at the first counter attack from the enemy? Or are you persistent, like the widow and the unjust judge? Overcoming the obstacles on your journey to your new level takes time and the enemies are ready to resist your progress.

> The walls do not normally fall in the first round; sometimes they fall in the thirteenth round.

> Ten plagues and countless visits to the palace by Moses were needed for the Pharaoh to let the people of Israel finally go.

Do you understand? It was the persistence of Joshua and Moses that snatched the victory. Only persistent and patient people, who insist, prevail, fight, try and try and try again, will see the day they conquer their obstacles and have victory over their enemies. Amen.

Chapter 5 Notes

(15) <u>You can reach the top</u> - Zig Ziglar - Cook Communications Ministries 2005 (p. 174)
(16) Cited in a conference by the Prophet Héctor Torres in the Apostolic and Prophetic Conference in Springfield, MA 2007
(17) Cited in a conference by the Apostle Alberto Guerrero at the Samarian Church in Madrid, Spain 2007

My Prayer

Lord, I ask you to give my dearest readers a new understanding so they may see and face the obstacles they will find on their way to a new level. Thank you because they have clear goals and have decided to press on. Thank you because we know you will use the obstacles they will face to reveal the best in them and form their character with meekness. I ask you that they could see how you glorify yourself in the midst of adversity and that they may not laugh like Sarah, but will rather trust in you as David did.

Help them fight the good battle as an excellent spiritual warrior that has control over all spiritual weapons. I pray they may be their own best friend and cheerleader, encouraging themselves in the most critical times. I pray for them to have a persistent spirit like Jacob and the widow who faced the unjust judge; that they be willing to walk the necessary times around the walls of Jericho for their obstacles and barriers to fall. That they may go in front of the Pharaoh as many times as needed until the Pharaoh releases what belongs to them. In Christ Jesus, we pray. Amen.

My Prophetic Declaration

- I declare my obstacles confirm that I am a visionary person with goals.

- I declare that each obstacle confirms that I am in the process of advancing and proceeding to my new season.

- I declare that each obstacle, instead of stopping me, will bring out all those things God has placed in me for that moment of adversity.

- I declare that in the midst of opposition and crisis, miracles and wonders will be released as well as the favor of God.

- I declare that opposition and crisis are opportunities for God to glorify himself in my life.

- I declare that like David, I will speak to myself, giving myself encouragement, and courage as many times needed. I declare myself my best friend, mentor, and cheerleader.

- I declare that, before my mountain of opposition, I will wage spiritual warfare. I will fight the good battle, like Paul, and I will use my spiritual weapons, which are powerful in God for the destruction of strongholds.

- I declare I am of a persistent spirit and I will insist as many times necessary, until I conquer the victory. Like Joshua, I will walk as many rounds as necessary. Like Moses, I will face my Pharaoh as many times as needed and like Jacob I will fight with the angel and I will not let him go until he blesses me. Amen.

VICIOUS CIRCLES

CHAPTER 6

"They soon forgot His works; they did not wait for
His counsel, but lusted exceedingly in the wilderness,
and tested God in the desert."

Psalm 106:13-14

We will never reach our new level if we continue to move in vicious circles. Many people are "in motion," but that in itself does not mean progress. Activity or busyness does not necessarily imply advancement. That I attend school does not guarantee that I am learning. That I go to work every day does not mean I am completing the tasks assigned to me. That on Sunday mornings I arrive to service does not automatically mean I am worshiping and receiving the Word of the Lord.

Activity does not mean advancement. What many people are doing instead is going in circles and more circles. They find themselves in the same place at the end of the year or at the end of a season in their lives. They moved during that time but did not advance. At first glance, it appears that you are advancing when you are really moving in circles. Before long, you return to the starting point. This is what I call the vicious circle, because you departed from the starting point but eventually return to the beginning – only to start all over again. Unless you break the cycle, in time you will return to the same place.

It must be terrifying to be detained, sitting, watching your opportunities pass by, instead of rising up and moving forward. It must be terrifying to have begun something only to leave it halfway, incomplete. Yet it must be even more terrifying to be moving, believing that you are advancing, when you are really only walking in circles. It must be frustrating to live with the illusion that you are advancing, when you are only moving in circles. What a way to lose your precious time! The sad aspect of all this is that many people deceive themselves believing that because they are moving, they are advancing.

> If you want to advance to your new level, you need to recognize you are trapped in a vicious circle. Then you need to break it and say in your heart of hearts: no more henceforth.

There are many people who are prisoners of their vicious circles, or suffer from as I call it the "Israel in the desert" syndrome. When we read the story of Israel from the time they leave Egypt under the direction of Moses until the time they arrive to the borders of the Promised Land, we see a people who demand action from God. In their first crisis, we see a people who demand God to act in their favor, and God does. Yet in their next crisis instead of trusting God, they complain, murmur, and doubt. Even then, God continually intervenes and supplies their every need. One might think they would have learned their lesson, yet in their next obstacle, we see the pattern repeat itself until they finally remain held up in the desert for years.

The psalmist describes in a very vivid manner that negative pattern, the vicious circles of the people of Israel. Read Psalm 106 and identify the vicious circles in verses 6-8, 10-12, 13-15, 16-17, 19-23, 24-26, 28-30, 32-33, 34-37 and 44-45. They were prisoners of their vicious circles that literally led them to walk in circles in the desert for 40 years. That generation never set foot in the Promised Land because they did not learn to break the vicious circle, that so dysfunctional pattern. The vicious circle turned their place of transition – the desert – into their place of inhabitance and in the end, their burial grounds.

> **Advancing to your new level requires that you be free from vicious circles.**

Vicious circles vary from one person to the next. For some, their vicious circles are their finances, for others it is their speech, yet for others it is how they handle their emotions, sexuality, temperament, self-esteem, discipline, self-control, and management of crisis.

The challenge for those who are imprisoned by the Israel syndrome is this: each time they face some of the areas mentioned above, they need to decide if they will face it acting in the same negative way of the past, or if they will break the vicious circle in a new, different, and positive way. This is what I call the **breaking point**, where instead of continuing to walk in circles, their walk is transformed into a straight line forward because of a new response to their challenge.

I want to tell you that the vicious circles – that dysfunctional pattern – can be broken. Receive these three pieces of advice to break those patterns and avoid having to go in any more circles.

First advice: Become tired of living in that state of being.

You need to reach a point where you do not want to go in any more circles. You need to reach the point where you decide you will not die in the desert, but instead will cross into the Promised Land. You need to reach the moment where you realize you are tired of being in the same place, doing the same things, and obtaining the same results. That attitude is very important since there are people who by force of habit accustom themselves to their dysfunction and do not desire to change nor exert themselves. You need to be convinced it is not enough to move, but that you desire to advance, to extend forward to what is ahead of you. You need to be completely decided to break the lifestyle of vicious circles.

Second advice: Recognize those areas in your life where you have been going around in circles.

Remember you can only fix something when you identify what has gone wrong. We will never resolve our problems if we do not identify them. There are people who recognize they have weak areas in their lives. However, when you ask them to list some of them, they cannot because they are only aware of the problem and not its cause. We need to move from the generic to the specific. It is not enough to say we have a problem in our marriage. We should rather add we have a communication problem. It is then that we can search for specific solutions because we have identified specific problems.

This appears easy but for many of us, it is not. It is not easy to identify our weak or dysfunctional areas because it turns out to be threatening, shameful, and painful. We need to overcome the pain and shame that result from looking at our mistakes, sins, and deficiencies. Many, to avoid the pain, hurt and shame, choose to deny or ignore their dysfunctional reality. They elect to turn their attentions to anything and everything except for their reality. We cover ourselves with denial when we are asked, "How are you?" and respond that all is well, knowing that our ship is sinking. We reach a point where we begin to believe our own lies. At times, we end up being the only ones who believe the lies making a fool out of ourselves since everyone knows our reality. We are the only ones who can confront and recognize our problems, mistakes, sins, and deficiencies. Many times, we decide to deny the truth. "Denial is ignoring the obvious," that is what is so ridiculous about denial.[18]

Others do not deny the truth, but rather choose to minimize it. They detract from its importance. It is much like that person whose house is on fire and they decide not to call the fire department because they have their own garden hose. The problem with that type of attitude is that the moment when they can no longer minimize their reality is the precise time when their garden hose is no longer sufficient to extinguish their fire – by that point, it is too late. No fire fighters in the area can save their home at that point.

It is important to understand that eventually our reality will catch up to us and manifest itself. It serves us best to confront our reality when there are opportunities to change it.

When we decide to deny or minimize our reality instead of confronting, identifying, and resolving it, we fall prey to a situation of alienation. Many people live in a state of alienation from their reality. You cannot move to your new level alienated or in denial about your reality. If you are like that, you will remain imprisoned and trapped in that condition. It is not the time to live in lies, fantasy, and illusion. We should rather recognize, confront, and overcome our realities, however painful they may be. The pain you will suffer that is caused by ignoring the situation will be greater and of broader impact than the pain caused by recognizing, confronting, and overcoming them in their due time.

If we want to recognize our weak areas, we need to overcome the barrier of pride. Pride paralyzes and impedes us from taking a stand and taking action with regard to our crisis. Pride makes us become more concerned with what others say, with our reputation and the opinion and judgment of other people than we do with the solution to our problems. There are people who prefer to continue in their dysfunctional pattern. There are people who prefer, rather than allow others to know their crises, to continue ill, going around in circles, never reaching their new level. Pride is a terrible thing that keeps us back in the place where we have always been and steals from us our best opportunities. Take the case of Naaman, commander of the army of the king of Syria (2nd Kings 5). He suffered from leprosy and so he went to the place where the Prophet Elisha was so he may be healed. Elisha gave him very clear and precise instructions for him to become clean of his leprosy. He orders Naaman to go to the Jordan and wash himself in it. Naaman was upset with the prophet because he understood the Jordan to be a filthy river, of second class that was not congruent with his stature, position, and image. Naaman knew and was accustomed to better rivers and in no way was he going to enter the Jordan.

Naaman's true problem was not his leprosy but rather his pride. Leprosy and the instructions the prophet gave him brought to the surface his real sickness: his pride. Because of his pride, he came close to losing the healing that would have improved his physical wellbeing. Many people prefer to lose their salvation than to come to the altar humbly to give their lives to the Lord. They give more importance to what the congregation might say when they see them come forward than to their salvation. Others prefer to die before they ask for prayer for some problem in their lives or before they ask for an appointment to be counseled on their crisis. There are many Naamans and Nicodemus in this time – those who desire help but want no one to know, no one to see them and as a result, they move in obscurity and shadows.

The prodigal son experienced a great failure but he had the valor to recognize his sin, his mistake, to call things by their name, confront his painful reality, assume responsibility for his actions, and return to his Father's house. Literally, the prodigal son swallowed his pride, but he also received restoration. He did not stay looking after pigs, desiring to eat husks, nor blaming his father for the rest of his life.

> **Overcome your pain and let go of your pride.**

As leaders, we have to overcome all of that pain and pride. "Confrontation doesn't always bring a solution to the problem, but until you confront the problem, there will be no solution."[19]

Every person has their crisis, their weak areas. There is no one exempt from this as we all have our issues. Each family has skeletons hidden in the closet that they have to confront. Do not give your reputation more value than the solution to your problems. Those watching are neither the ones living with you nor the ones having to confront what you are going through. Think about the wellbeing that you will have when you find a solution to your crisis and when you overcome the weak areas in your life. Think that, instead of going around in circles, you can begin to transform your circle into a straight line forward. Think about the new level that you will reach.

Third advice: Find adequate help.
Seeking adequate help to come out of your depth and crisis is not a bad thing. There was a time when people thought those who went to see a therapist, counselor, pastor, or psychologist were either crazy or mentally ill. This is a false belief. That I need help does not necessarily mean that I am mentally deranged. At times, it becomes necessary to seek external help when we feel trapped in a diverse set of situations and we cannot see our way forward. We cannot resolve all situations by ourselves every single time.

I want to tell you that God, in his mercy and divine providence, has provided quality help for you. In fact, that assistance is closer than you think. It is close; in fact perhaps too close which is why you may not be able to discern it. You know something:

- There are people who drown in the high seas next to a ship with life vests.
- There are people who die of hunger next to a well-stocked warehouse.
- There are people who cannot find medicines inside a pharmacy.
- There are people who cannot see nor identify their help.

> **God has placed key people near you to bless you, help you, and thrust you forward to your new level.**

God has sent key people close to you to bless you, help you, and propel you to your new level. God has placed people like your pastors, spiritual leaders, some family members, and friends who are willing to invest time in you. They are willing to listen to you, pray with you, counsel you, and keep you company throughout your crisis. Do not ignore them any longer. Go to them and let them help you. Let go of all your defense mechanisms and make yourself vulnerable to them. You need to trust in someone so let them help you and let go of your fears.

Not only are there key people who will help you, there are also events to which you can attend so you may obtain the tools and skills needed to overcome your weak areas and break the vicious circles in your life. You cannot stay locked up in your room, crying your way out your crisis, feeling sorry for yourself, and lamenting over what will happen. There are events and seminars that will train, teach, inspire, and counsel you. You should attend events or conferences designed to help you come out of the depths you are in and move you to a new level. Do your homework, ask around, and if you find something you need, then register yourself for those events and seminars, attend, and expose yourself.

Begin with the worship and preaching services each Sunday. Maximize the word that the Lord is giving your pastor. Maximize the time of worship during the service. Join those who during worship exalt God in the midst of their crisis. Attend the prayer services and open your heart to the Lord like Anna, Samuel's mother (1st Samuel 1:9-12). Attend conferences in the area that can contribute to your growth in your weak areas. Read good books and see TV shows or videos of anointed preachers, people prepared in the topics where you need help. In the end, do not stay all by yourself at the level where you recognize your problem, but rather seek spiritual and professional help that is able and capable to assist you in your need.

The prodigal son not only recognized his problem but he also sought help to resolve the same. That is why he moved from his environment and changed the persons with which he was relating since he understood they could not help him. In fact, those people were part of his problem. He left a promiscuous environment and returned to his Father's house.

> Identify positive environments and people who you should associate with, embrace them, and flee from bad influence and contaminated environments.

The prodigal son once again sought the covering of his Father and he distanced himself from his so-called friends. Your restoration cannot take place in just any place and with just any one. There are people who have been established by God in certain places and positions, with certain abilities to help you. Identify them, seek them out, place yourself under their covering, and ask for their help.

Jacob's story

Jacob's story is one filled with hope, especially for those who for years have been imprisoned in vicious circles. This story demonstrates you can come out of your dysfunctional patterns and the vicious circles can be broken. The message Jacob gives us is this: you do not have reason to go around in circles all your life, you do not have to live fleeing, and you do not have to die in the desert.

Jacob spent a great part of his life resolving his crises in a negative way. When he found himself in a crisis, he would flee from it, either by deceiving others or by lying. It was in this way that he earned his name: the deceiver, the supplanter. He did such with his brother Esau, he also deceived his father, and he fled from his family. Later, in Padan Aram, he continues with his tricks and deceits in the house of his uncle Laban who in his own right was not too far behind Jacob in his traps and deceitfulness. After many years, Jacob leaves the house of Laban in Padan Aram to return to Canaan.

If we study the story carefully, we can identify and see in action the three advices we shared earlier to break the vicious circle.

1) Jacob grows tired of his lifestyle Genesis 31:17
We see Jacob decide to return to his family and confront his reality instead of fleeing from it. He literally grew tired of that state of being.

2) Jacob recognized his problem Genesis 32:27
When the angel asks his name, he responds as Jacob, the deceiver, liar, and supplanter. This has been my problem, my struggle, my weak area. He called things by their name. Though it was painful and shameful, he did not cover his weakness.

3) Jacob sought help to change Genesis 32:26-28
Jacob begins to struggle with the angel, and in a persistent manner tells him: you have to help me. I will not let you go if you do not bless me. I will not let you go until you change my name. I no longer want to be Jacob. Set loose my new name – Israel. Jacob identified his help and did not let his opportunity pass by.

That morning, Jacob was changed to Israel. We can see the immediate transformation in his life since in his next crisis, instead of fleeing, he confronts his brother Esau and reconciles with him.

I have news for you. You do not have to live your entire life being a Jacob – you can be an Israel. To advance to your new level you need to leave Jacob behind and transform into an Israel. Jacob did not transform himself; the angel, embodiment of Christ, was the one who transformed Jacob into Israel. The transformation was the labor of the angel. Jacob had only to desire it wholeheartedly. Christ is the one who changes, delivers, and transforms. His power is available. Now one question remains: is there today a Jacob who has the desire, the courage, and audacity to ask God to transform him?

There is a Peniel awaiting you. You do not need to go in any more vicious circles.

Chapter 6 Notes

(18) <u>You can reach the top</u> - Zig Ziglar - Cook Communications Ministries 2005 (p. 172)

(19) <u>You can reach the top</u> - Zig Ziglar - Cook Communications Ministries 2005 (p. 146)

My Prayer

Lord, I am in one accord with my readers, so that at this time in their lives they decide to break all vicious circles that have been holding them back in their walk towards a new level. I pray so they do not go one more circle in their walk. I pray you give them the strength of will to see the weak areas in their life so they may overcome all pain, shame, and pride; that they may confront their reality and transform it. I pray they may be willing to receive the help needed.

I ask their spiritual eyes be opened so they may identify those people who can help them. That the assistance they receive be effective, positive, and that it guides them to transform their circles into straight shots forward. That they may move from environments that feed their dysfunctional patterns. That they may be able to let go of the negative people in their lives so they can reach the places you have separated for them. That they might find and relate themselves with key people who will help propel them to their new level. I pray so there may be a Peniel in the life of my dear reader, where *Jacob* dies and *Israel* is born. In Christ Jesus, we pray. Amen.

My Prophetic Declaration

- I declare I am tired of going around in circles without really advancing.

- I declare I will cease to go around in circles so I may walk towards my new level.

- I declare I will recognize my weak areas and all dysfunctional patterns that want to hold me up in my transitory place.

- I declare I will not be afraid to confront my reality and identify it, though it may cause me pain and shame. I will not become alienated nor will I live in lies.

- I declare I will not let my pride steal my new level. I refuse to be a Nicodemus or a Naaman.

- I declare, that as the prodigal son, I will leave the limiting environments and negative people in my life so I may go to my Father's house. That I will be under his covering and will be restored and taught by him.

- I declare I do not have to fear asking for and receiving help from the people who the Lord has set aside for me.

- I declare I will go to my divine appointment in Peniel and I will not let pass my opportunity to be delivered from my *Jacob* and to give birth to my *Israel*. I will fight, ask for, plead, and insist until sunrise if I have to but under no conditions will I accept going in circles any longer.

- I declare I am free to move forward and continue to my new level.

INTIMATE CIRCLE
CHAPTER 7

"He who walks with the wise grows wise, but a companion of fools suffers harm."

Proverbs 13:20 (NIV)

Another factor to consider if we want to advance to our new level is to evaluate who makes up our intimate circle. There is a powerful connection between the advancing or progressing of a person and the makeup of their intimate circle. The people whom we associate with can bless us or curse us, can push us forward or detain us, can advance us or retain us. There is power in relationships.

There are two things that caught my attention in Prophet Silvana Armentano's book, "Mujeres de Poder," (Women of Power)[20] when she addressed the power of relationships. In the first place, she compares interpersonal relationships with an elevator. Some relationships, just like an elevator, can take you to the penthouse, but others to the basement. Some relationships bring you up, while others take you down. I ask you, who have you allowed into the elevator of your life? What floors have they selected for you? Are you ascending or descending? Maybe on your next stop, you should ask some of them to get off your elevator because they are selecting lower floors for you when your goal is to ascend.

Armentano also says that everyone we establish a relationship with will sow a seed in us and, in its due time, those seeds will bear fruit. Somehow, those seeds will affect our thinking, our words, our vision, and our actions. Those seeds will leave trails, signs, and influences in our lives, whether intentional or not.[21] The point we should examine is this: what kind of seed will a person sow in me? You should know that not all seeds bear the same fruit. Remember: "he who sows winds will reap storms;" he who sows in the flesh will reap corruption. If you are determined to go to your new level, you cannot allow everyone to sow in your heart. You will have to examine carefully each sower and his or her seed.

> He who is advancing to higher levels cares for his heart, because he knows that he is a special person, with a calling and a divine destiny. He knows that he cannot allow just anyone to get in his elevator (his life) or sow in his land (his heart).

One thing is to have too much company and have to choose from them those who will propel you to your new level, and it is quite another to be alone. God's plan has never been for you to be alone, to work alone, to fight alone, or to reach your victories alone. The preacher clarifies this point for us.

> "Two are better than one, because they have a good return for their work: If one falls down, his friend can help him up. But pity the man who falls and has no one to help him up! Also, if two lie down together, they will keep warm. But how can one keep warm alone? Though one may be overpowered, two can defend themselves. A cord of three strands is not quickly broken." Ecclesiastes 4:9-12 (NIV)

You need others in order to reach your goals and your purposes. I like what Dr. John Maxwell says about this: "Although you may be able to take the journey without others, I can tell you that you will never be able to reach your maximum potential and go to the highest level if you take the journey alone. Over time I've learned this meaningful lesson: The people closest to me determine my level of success or failure."[22] Maxwell reminds us that we cannot go to the next level or reach the divine calling in our lives alone. In this journey, we need the support of others at different stages of our lives. Let us understand this truth: **we cannot make the journey to new levels alone.**

On the other hand, simply having company beside you will not guarantee you success in your journey upwards. It depends on the type of people who you choose to accompany you and the kind of seed they will sow in you. That is why Maxwell says those closest to you have the power to determine your success or your failure. That declaration is too powerful to ignore. I cannot be with just anyone. This requires a level of discernment, an intentional, conscious, and conscientious process. I cannot delegate to others to choose those who have the power to push me forward or to hold me back.

It is vital to know and discern whom you associate yourself with, whom you open your heart to, and who your mentors are. The wisdom writer declared it is not the same to walk with wise men than with fools as the result will be different. When we associate ourselves with wise people, we will be wise, but when our intimate circle is composed of fools, the results will be poor and cause us to suffer harm. **No one can go to a new level in such a condition.**

> "He who walks with the wise grows wise, but a companion of fools suffers harm."
>
> Proverbs 13:20 (NIV)

Intimate Circle

Who am I referring to when I speak of the intimate circle? Obviously, in life we relate with an immense number of people. We relate with people at our jobs, in our neighborhood, at our churches, in other social institutions, on our way to the supermarket, in the bank, and at the airport terminal; but these people do not automatically make up our intimate circle.

When we speak about a circle, we are already saying that there is a reduction in the number of people who qualify. It is not a multitude; it is a select group of people. When we say intimate, we are speaking about very close people with whom we can establish a deeper and quality relationship. With them, we will speak about topics and we will share issues that are not aired publicly.

> Many focus on the amount of people they associate with, but the focus should be on quality not quantity.

The intimate circle is composed of people very close to you, those whom you open your heart to, those you entrust with your dreams, visions, goals, and callings. They are people with whom you share your battles, doubts, questions, and failures, knowing that you can trust them and they are not going to cause you harm. They are people with whom you share quality time, with whom you can learn, grow, and mature. They are your true friends, mentors, spiritual mothers, and fathers. They want you to carry out your divine calling, not take advantage of you. That is why not everyone qualifies to be part of your intimate circle.

King Ahab was unsuccessful in his kingship, in part, because of his decision to marry Jezebel, a pagan woman and a sorcerer who took control over his kingdom's power and drove it to failure. In the same way, King Solomon almost deviated from his faith by taking foreign and pagan women as his wives. **The closest people to us can advance us to success or failure.**

- Imagine a person who has "bad credit," full of debts, and wants to get out of it, but their intimate circle is composed of people in debt, with failures, people who are bankrupt and still live in that vicious circle.

- Imagine a person who wants to improve the quality of their job, get a promotion and a raise, but associates with those co-workers who are irresponsible, the ones who are late to work, and who avoid doing their job.

- Imagine a student who hopes to graduate from high school with excellent grades but is always with students who do not do their homework, who disrespect their teachers, skip their classes, and spend half of their day at the principal's office or suspended altogether.

- Imagine a Christian person who desires to grow in their relationship with God, in their faith, and in their ministry, but their intimate circle is composed of brethren who get to church late, only go on Sundays, who sit in the back of the church, who fall asleep during the preaching, and who gossip about the pastor.

How can these people advance and overcome their obstacles with those kinds of associations and influences in their lives?

The intimate circle of the paralytic from Capernaum

The Capernaum paralytic was able to achieve his goal. He was able to receive healing, a miracle from Jesus, thanks to his intimate circle. He knew how to choose his friends. Thanks to these four friends, he was able to get to where Jesus was, get through the crowd, and descend from the roof. The paralytic was definitely a man of faith and his friends were as well. Look at what Mark 2:5 says "**When Jesus saw their faith...**" It was not only the faith of the paralytic that stood out, but also the faith of the friends who carried him.

It was a team of faith; all five of them were people of faith, not just the paralytic. His friends paid attention to his request, they did not laugh at him, they did not deny him help, they did not abandon him in front of the crowd, and they took a risk when they raised the paralytic to the roof. The paralytic alone could have not done it, but thanks to the quality of his intimate circle, he was able to achieve it and in that manner, he moved to a new time in his life. Your intimate circle will make a difference in your life.

Moses and his intimate circle

When Moses faced the Amalekites, he decided to go to the top of the hill and cry out to God while Joshua led the battle on the valley. But Moses did not go up alone; Aaron and Hur went with him. They took care of Moses and when Moses' knees and arms were tired of interceding they sat him on a rock and held his arms up until Joshua and the people prevailed and obtained the victory (Exodus 17:8-13). Moses' intimate circle supported him until they reached the victory.

Imagine if Moses had gone to the hill by himself or had chosen carelessly two other people to go with him. For example, if he had chosen Korah and Dathan, who were two of the leaders that led an uprising against Moses; they might have thrown him over the edge.

Someone expanded on the saying, "tell me who you walk with and I will tell you who you are," this way, "tell me who you walk with and I will tell you how far you will go." I would add: "tell me who you walk with and I will tell you where you will be a year from now, five years from now." Remember: those closest to you will determine your success or failure.

> **The reason for stagnation and low productivity for many is the kind of people with whom they relate.**

There is a high price to pay when you join people who are depressed, self-conscious, with failures, bitter, without a vision, conformists, and mediocre. It is crucial you pause and review who you are walking with and who constitutes your intimate circle. It is necessary that you evaluate the effect and contribution these people are imparting on you. Leader, check who you are associating yourself with and who you are walking with.

You will be amazed at what you will discover when you review and evaluate with whom you associate. It is possible you will have to make some changes and end some relationships to be able to advance to your new level. Do not look at it as something out of the norm.

> **God has separated different people, in different seasons of our lives to instruct us in different areas.**

I heard someone once say the people who started with us, as part of our team, are not necessarily those who will end with us. This does not mean they are negative people. Their time in our lives simply ended. They finished their assignment and it is someone else's turn to follow up with us. It is very important to know when to make these changes and whom we choose, because no one who is at or below your level can bring you to new levels.

Not too long ago I read the experience of the Christian writer John Mason[23] regarding the people with whom he associated himself with and I identified with his story. He says:

> "A number of years ago I found myself at a stagnation point in my life; I was unproductive and unable to see God's direction clearly. One day I noticed that almost all of my friends were in the same situation. When we got together, our problems were what we talked about. As I prayed about this matter, God showed me that I needed 'foundation-level' people in my life ... The Lord showed me that I needed to change my closest associations and that I needed to have contact with the right people on a regular basis. These were men of strong faith, people who made me a better person when I was around them. They were the ones who saw the gifts in me and could correct me in a constructive, loving way. My choice to change my closest associations was a turning point in my life."

This was also my experience. For a while, I was ascending in my ministry, but there came a time in my life when I was not advancing. I was only maintaining the successes and levels already achieved; there were no new challenges. When the Lord shook me out of the comfort of my boat and called me to deep waters, to walk on water; the first objections and obstacles came, not from outside, but from those close to me. Good people, nevertheless people who lived too comfortable with the past and with their then-current level of faith. They were not planning to leave the shore or the boat in the midst of an angry sea.

I was able to realize their particular work from God in my life had ended. This in no way minimizes the relationship that I had with them because they were key people who had raised me to the level I was currently in and they had blessed my ministry in a powerful way. I will forever be grateful and I hold nothing against them, only a debt of gratitude. As I write the story of my life, I have to mention them, because I consider them a gift from God. However, continuing in these relationships could have cost me my new level.

When we fall in love with our blessing more than with He who blesses us, we can fall behind. When we fall in love with the glory of where we currently are, we could lose the new level of glory. We have to be cautious about this because many things in our lives are transitional or temporary, but the calling and our fidelity to God is of eternal character.

Abraham was close to losing his calling, his blessing, and his destiny when he insisted in taking Lot, his orphan nephew, when God had told him: "Leave your house and your people." It was not until they parted ways and ended with the level and type of relationship they had grown accustomed to that God's plan with Abraham entered a new level. Abraham's relationship with Lot was making him fall behind. Abraham had already carried out his promise to his brother. Lot was no longer a child or a young man; he was an adult who had to assume control and responsibility for his life. The end of this relationship did not mean Abraham would forget about his nephew. He continued to relate with Lot, but in a different way. Do you understand the nuances there?

There was a time when two millionaire friends who had not seen each other in a few years met up. While they were catching up, the first one told the second one that he was now a billionaire. This surprised the second one because he had become a millionaire before his friend. Also, this second one had tried without succees for the last couple of years to become a billionaire. When the second asked how he did it, the first responded by asking him whom he was associating with, to which the second one responded: millionaires, we are all millionaires. The first noted: "That's what you're doing wrong; you need to find yourself some billionaires and begin associating with them! They'll get you thinking at their level."[24] It was evident the billionaires knew things the millionaires did not know, that is why they were already billionaires.

Moral of the story: if you want to be a billionaire, stop walking with millionaires. In other words, if you want to go up to your new level, begin to associate yourself with the people from the next level. You have to grow closer to wise men and women who know more than you do, who are at higher level than you are, so they can make significant impartations in your life. We are talking about people of success, people on the mountaintop, eagle-like people, of faith, knowledge, experience, maturity, and integrity. They are people who will bring out the best in you and will challenge you; people who have gone through the fire, through the many waters, who have crossed the valley of tears, who have faced giants, and have moved mountains. Do you know what I am talking about?

> **We need to connect with people who have experience, marks in their spirit, people who have gone through significant processes in their lives, and now have something to say; not with people who only have or know the theory.**

I heard Bishop T.D. Jakes in one of his sermons on television say: "If in the circle in which you move you are the one who always talks, the one who knows most, who everyone looks to, your circle is too limited."[25] Without turning your back on this circle, you need to join a circle where you will not be the one who talks or teaches all the time, but the one who listens, who takes notes, the one who asks, and learns. If you are surrounded by those who know the same or less than you do, it will be difficult for you to learn and expand.

Mentors

To be able to go to your new level, in addition to a meaningful intimate circle, you need good mentors or spiritual parents. The story of the Prophet Elisha cannot be described without mentioning the main role his mentor and spiritual father Elijah had. In the same manner, Joshua became who he was thanks to his spiritual father Moses. Timothy and Titus, two young pastors, were influenced and formed by his mentor and spiritual father, the Apostle Paul.

Nowadays, our individualistic society has marginalized the role of the mentor and the spiritual mother or father. Thanks to God, we are seeing a restoration in the ministry of the mentor and of the spiritual father in the Church. Without the mentor ministry and spiritual paternity, the new generation will stay in the same level in which they are now. How will they move to places they have not seen and do not know they even exist?

Every mentor and spiritual father has the commitment to leave an inheritance and a spiritual impartation to its generation. They need to align their generation, pass the baton, and boost their sons and daughters to their destiny.

It is a disgrace for a mentor or spiritual father to die taking with them everything they have and know without leaving behind a Joshua or Timothy. It is a greater disgrace when none of the sons or protégées is interested in receiving the father's impartation. I believe the actual crisis rests more in the absence or lack of interest in the Elishas, Joshuas, and Timothies of today. They think they can make it on their own, without the help of mentors or spiritual parents.

Teaching on the subject of the mentor, Mike Murdock says that mentors are teachers of wisdom and he makes mention of twelve truths regarding the importance and role of mentors. One of them is that the mentor is the *master* key for the success of their protégée.[26] It serves you well to understand that the role of your mentor or spiritual parent is not to give you comfort, since that can be left up to your friends. Your mentor seeks to push you towards your calling and purpose. I like how Mike Murdock pens it:

"An uncommon mentor is more interested in your success than your affection. His focus is not the celebration of you, but, the correction of you." [27]

It is fundamental to know this principle to maximize the ministry of your spiritual parents.

> **Some spiritual sons only flow when their father or mentor pushes, motivates, feeds, or introduces them to new environments, but as soon as the father or mentor corrects, disciplines, or confronts them, they turn their backs on them, they cease to recognize their authority, they criticize them, and fire them.**

It is dangerous to be surrounded by people who only tell you how good you are, who talk about the way you do things well, and affirm your strengths. We need to find that mentor, that spiritual parent who will adopt us, love us, form us, and will have the freedom to point out our mistakes, our sins, our weak areas, and where we need to improve. The purpose is not to damage our self-esteem nor is it to destroy us. On the contrary, their purpose is to help us reach our new level and carry out our divine assignment. Those closest to you will determine your success or your failure.

John Mason[28] reminds us these brief thoughts:

- If you run with wolves, you will learn to howl, but if you associate with eagles, you will learn how to soar to great heights.
- If you find yourself taking two steps forward and one step backwards, invariably it is because you have mixed associations in your life.
- Keep out of the suction caused by those who drift backwards.
- Look carefully at your closest associates, because it is an indication of the direction you are heading.

Chapter 7 Notes

(20) Mujeres de Poder (Women of Power) - Silvana Armentano - Editorial Adoradores Unidos 2003 (p. 105)

(21) Mujeres de poder (Women of Power) - Silvana Armentano - Editorial Adoradores Unidos 2003 (p. 106-107)

(22) Your Road Map For Success - John Maxwell - Nelson Business 2002 (p. 186)

(23) The Impossible Is Possible: Doing What Others Say Can't Be Done - John Mason - Bethany House Publishers 2003 (p. 33)

(24) Thinking for a Change - John Maxwell – First Warner Books 2003 (p. 34)

(25) Conference by the Bishop T.D. Jakes – daily TV program "The Potter's House" - TBN TV 2005

(26) The Law of Recognition - Mike Murdock - Wisdom International 1999 (p. 33-35)

(27) The Law of Recognition - Mike Murdock - Wisdom International 1999 (p. 34)

(28) The Impossible Is Possible: Doing What Others Say Can't Be Done - John Mason - Bethany House Publishers 2003 (p. 32-34)

My Prayer

God Almighty, I ask that my dear readers may understand the truths of this chapter. I ask that they can understand the importance of the people they associate with. I ask that you help them to evaluate their intimate circle with integrity. Give them the courage to make the necessary changes in order to ascend to their next level.

God, allow them to find and associate with the mentors that you have for them in this season of their lives. Allow them to value their spiritual parents and to receive the impartation they have for them. Help them to be mentors and spiritual parents for the Elijahs and Timothies you have put under them. In Christ Jesus, we pray. Amen.

My Prophetic Declaration

- I declare that as the paralytic from Capernaum and Moses, I know how to choose those who make up my intimate circle.

- I declare that I will identify, value, and associate with the people God has set apart to be my mentors in this season of my life.

- I declare I will voluntarily submit to my spiritual parents in order to receive the inheritance from them and the impartation of the things I need to go to my new level.

- I declare I will walk with the wise instead of the fools.

- I declare I am a Joshua, an Elisha, and a Timothy. I walk in harmony with my Moses, my Elijah, and my Paul.

- I declare that with God's favor, I will be an Elijah and a Paul for those who I can influence and protect so they can also advance to their next level.

- I declare I will not take to the grave what I have received from God; instead, I will impart it unto others.

STRATEGIES

CHAPTER 8

"And the LORD said to Joshua: 'See! I have given Jericho into your hand, its king, and the mighty men of valor. You shall march around the city, all you men of war; you shall go all around the city once. This you shall do six days.'"

Joshua 6:2-3

To move to your new level you will need new and specific strategies from God. He is interested in your movement into a new level. He wants you to continue your advancement in your walk of faith. That is why he wants to give you the instructions, methods, and strategies so you can move on and advance. We cannot assume that the strategies of the past are going to work automatically with God's plan for our lives. Just because some strategies worked in the past, it does not mean they are going to work today. We need to be very careful that we do not idolize the strategies and try to use old strategies that are no longer working on circumstances; circumstances that need new and fresh methods.

> **The biblical principles and statutes of the kingdom of God do not change through the ages, but the strategies and methods do change.**

When we talk about God's strategies, we need to establish that they will never violate any biblical ethics or morals. Not all wars are fought the same ways. Not all goals are attained in the same way. The end perhaps does not change but the means by which we attain them may. Many people insist on using archaic and old methods today. On the other hand, there are people using new and fresh strategies and obtaining great results from them. That is not the only criteria we should use. I have to discover the strategies God has for me. Proverbs 20:18 says.

"... By wise counsel wage war ..."

Wise council means that we choose the strategies and methods with wisdom and intelligence. Remember this: you cannot arrive at your destiny improvising or imitating the plans and strategies of others. You most certainly will need strategies that are exclusively for you. These only come from God.

We need specific strategies from God.

We need to recognize that our strategies are not always the best. Sometimes when we think something is a certain way, it turns out to be another, and what we may at times think is not the right way turns out to be exactly what we have to do. Our perspective and views are limited, that is why we need divine intervention. Let us remember how certain Samuel was when he went to anoint the next king of Israel and was selecting from the sons of Jesse. God warns him from the beginning only to anoint the one He tells him to anoint. When Samuel saw Jesse's first son Eliab, he says: "Surely the Lord's anointed is before Him!"

Samuel was impressed and arrived at a quick conclusion because of Eliab's stature and good looks, but the Lord had to intervene and say to him that he was wrong: "For *the LORD does* not *see* as man sees; for man looks at the outward appearance, but the LORD looks at the heart." (1st Samuel 16:1-7).

We cannot choose our methods and strategies solely based on what we see and know, happened in the past, or are the current trends and fads. We should turn to God so that He can give us the strategies to overcome our obstacles.

The Lord gave specific strategies to:
- Moses about freeing God's people from the Pharaoh.
- Joshua on conquering the Promised Land.
- Gideon about overcoming the Midianites.
- Esther on how to save the Jewish people from certain death.
- David on how to conquer the giant.
- Nehemiah on restoring the city.
- Paul on how to bring forward the Gospel to the gentiles.

What is the difference between Moses and Paul, David and Gideon? He gave Moses a staff; He reduced Gideon's army from 32,000 to 300 people and a handful of cooking pots. To king Jehoshaphat, He orders the Levites and musicians be placed in the front. He tells Nehemiah to form different teams. He gives detailed instructions to Joshua during a seven-day campaign to bring down the walls of Jericho. Paul and Silas are told simply to dedicate themselves to prayer and singing during their imprisonment at Philippi. These were powerful strategies, each unique to their circumstances, and yet effective strategies for each person and each moment. Paul could not copy Joshua's strategies nor could Nehemiah copy Gideon's. Everyone followed and flowed with the strategies God had for them.

> **It is vital to know and obey God's divine strategies so that we can move to our next level.**

I want to share some simple yet practical principles about how to receive the specific strategies God has for you.

1) You should learn how to listen and discern God's voice.

God still speaks. He has not lost the capacity to communicate with His children. We can still say as the child Samuel said in the temple: "Speak Lord that your servant is listening." It is important to know how to listen and distinguish God's voice from the voice of the enemy, people, your ego, and your emotions. Jesus continues to call out his sheep to follow him. Therefore, as children of God we need to know our Father's voice. In order to learn how to listen to his voice and receive what he has in store for you, you must:

a) Spend time with the word

You need to be completely submerged with the Word of God. You need to read, memorize, meditate, speak, treasure it in your heart, and put it to practice. It is important that we study the word of God because they reveal the heart of God. Jesus said the following:

> "You diligently study the Scriptures because you think that by them you possess eternal life. These are the Scriptures that testify about me."
>
> John 5:39

Do not expect God to speak continually to you in an audible voice if you are overlooking the daily, formal, serious, and deep study of the Word of God. Remember that the prophetic word, *rhema*, is founded in the *logos* word.

If we want to learn how to listen to the voice of God to receive the strategies you also need to:

b) Have communion with the beloved Holy Spirit

Who better to help us than the Holy Spirit who knows all things and whom God has given us to help in our mission? The Holy Spirit desires to reveal the secret things of God to us.

> "We have not received the spirit of the world but the Spirit who is from God, that we may understand what God has freely given us."
>
> 1st Corinthians 2:12

The work of the Holy Spirit is to teach us and remind us the Word, guide us to all truth and justice, give us revelation, visions, dreams, and prophetic utterance. Hallelujah! (Read John 14:26, John 16:12-15 and Acts 2:17-18). In the third place, to hear and discern the voice of God you need to:

c) Spend time in His presence

You need to set time apart to be with Him, enjoy Him, and have intimacy with Him. You need time to worship and exalt Him as in Psalm 63. When we set aside quality time with Him, without any rush, God will open His heart to us and will show us that which we need to know. Among other things, He will give us strategies to conquer our Jericho, our Goliaths, and the Midianites.

- To be good listeners we need to learn to be still (Psalm 46:10). People who are electric and constantly moving cannot pay the needed attention and will surely miss the most important moments. **Be still!**

- To be good listeners we need to learn how to be quiet. While we are talking, we are not listening. You need to be silent to hear God's voice and what He is trying to say. You need to be set free from Job's syndrome of talking, talking, and not being silent (Job 42:3). "But the LORD is in His holy temple. Let all the earth keep silence before Him" (Habakkuk 2:20). **Be quiet!**

- To be a good listener of God you need to congregate in your church. You need to pay attention to the word being preached and the exhortation of your pastor and spiritual leaders. God also uses them to give you a specific word and instructions. **Congregate!**

Remember what the book of Hebrews says:

> "Let us not give up meeting together, as some are in the habit of doing, but let us encourage one another and all the more as you see the Day approaching."
> Hebrews 10:25

> "Remember your leaders, who spoke the word of God to you. Consider the outcome of their way of life and imitate their faith."
> Hebrews 13:7

Guard yourself from moving from church to church, service to service, and prophet to prophet; looking for God to speak to you while you are at the same time despising and neglecting your church and your spiritual leaders. This dangerous practice of hopping around opens the door to spirits of falsehood.

Be careful with loose prophets and dark places that are not accountable to anyone and minister without their pastors knowing it. Guard yourself against the pseudo-prophets that seek people to prophesy to and are doing it not in the spirit but in the flesh. Prophets who tell you what you want to hear, what they already know, and who are used by the enemy to confuse you and fill you with fear.

Be careful with those alleged prophets, who are none other than wizards and fortunetellers operating under familiar spirits. There are no quick and easy formulas in the Lord. Invest time in His presence. Have communion with the Holy Spirit. Study His Word. Attend your church, congregate, and receive the Word in every message. Go to your discipleship meetings. Value your pastor and leaders. Discern the prophecies and test the prophets evaluating, discerning, and receiving confirmation of their words.

2) You need to be willing to obey the instructions the Lord has given you.

Once you know it was God who spoke to you and gave you His strategies, the next step is to obey and execute. Many invest time asking God to speak to them, but once He reveals His plans they do not execute them and instead scrap the plans. Many do not obey because they do not like the strategies, instructions, or orders they were given. It was not what they were hoping for; the plan or idea they had sounded better than God's plans.

If you are not willing to obey what God reveals to you, do not waste His time asking Him to speak to you.

Knowledge without obedience leads to wasted time. Of what value is revelation without action? Knowing what God wants and sends you to do is good, but it is more important to do what He asks of you. God does not bless your intelligence, He blesses your obedience. Knowing God's strategy is not what gives you the victory, but rather implementing the strategy is what propels you to your new level. When you obey, you are promoted to the next level.

When you receive visions and dreams from God and share them with others, you will receive glory; people will see you as someone who is blessed and special, someone out of this world. Nevertheless, obedience to God's instructions for you – perhaps given in dreams or visions – will many times bring with it criticism, pain, and enemies.

Obedience implies paying the price. It is to place oneself under pressure. One example of this is King Saul. Because he did not want to have the people against him and wanted to keep them content, He disobeyed God's instructions and instead did what the people told him. He preserved animals, people, and treasures that God had told him to destroy. It was a costly mistake.

> **The problem with many people is not the lack of revelation, but rather the lack of obedience.**

Peter and John could have easily evaded many of the incarcerations and beatings if they ceded to the request of the scribes and priests. They were only asked to stop preaching and talking about Christ. Nevertheless, Peter and John firmly said:

> "...But Peter and John replied, 'Judge for yourselves whether it is right in God's sight to obey you rather than God. For we cannot help speaking about what we have seen and heard.'"　　　　　Acts 4:19-20

There is a cost to obedience. It is much easier to receive the revelation than to obey it. When the Lord gives you the strategies to bring you to the next level in your calling and ministry, obey it, and obey it exactly as it is given to you. Do not change, alter, or modify any of the instructions or strategies God has given you. Simply move in God's *kairos*, in his perfect time, neither before nor after the precise time.

The maturity of a believer is demonstrated in their capacity to obey God's ordinances whether they like them or even understand them. Visions, dreams, or even angelic apparitions do not demonstrate your spirituality. That may impress others, but not God. God is impressed and pleased with your obedience. What does it really matter if you tell me with the finest of details what God has told you, or what you felt, or how the room was filled with smoke, or how you saw God's presence, or how angels moved around you if you are living in disobedience? What is it worth if you have yet to do what God has told you to do? Suspend your tour of testimonies and your conferences about angelical encounters. First, concentrate on obeying what he has ordered you to do.

What would have happened if the virgin Mary had told the angel that she liked the vision and calling but that she did not want to get pregnant? The amazing thing in this narration is seen in Luke 1:26-38 when she finally says "I am the Lord's servant … May it be to me as you have said." She accepted the challenge, the strategy from God and the consequences of obedience.

3) To carry out and realize God's strategies requires a willingness to appear ridiculous in the eyes of others.

Christians who are more worried about their image and reputation than obedience to God will have problems. If you are more worried about being accepted and about what others think about you than about God's opinion, then you will have a hard time obeying and realizing the strategies God will give you. Why? Because many strategies will make you look ridiculous in the eyes of people who are not Christians or in front of carnal Christians.

- Can you imagine Elisha waiting with his silverware at the ready for the crows that were bringing him food? Can you picture him later on responding when someone asked him where he was going: "I am going to Zarephath to the house of a widow and her son who only have a portion of flour so they can feed me until the drought finishes." Elisha had no other choice but to do the ridiculous because that was the strategy God had given him. He did not die of hunger but rather ate well when no one else had anything to eat.

- Can you imagine Moses, with the Pharaoh's army behind him, the Red Sea in front, and with the people looking at him waiting for him to say something? It was then when Moses extended his staff – old, dry, and unimposing – so the waters would separate. That was the strategy from God, and it worked because the people of Israel crossed on dry land.

- Can you imagine Gideon preparing to go to war with only 300 people, having just released 31,700 soldiers instead of recruiting more? Can you imagine Gideon passing old pots and torches out as they surrounded the numerous Midianite armies? But the strategy worked. Gideon and his 300 soldiers tasted the victory that with the thirty-two thousand soldiers they would not have had.

- What do you say about the young man David who was taking care of sheep and killed Goliath with a sling shot while the astonished King Saul and his army were watching? Goliath himself did not believe it. It was ridiculous. But you know what? The strategy worked and Goliath was history a few minutes later.

- Can I mention Paul and Silas in the jail at Philippi? They were beaten, chained, and preparing for the worst the next day. They followed God's strategy of singing hymns and praying to God. Anyone who heard them and saw them would think they were crazy. Guess what? The strategy worked and they were freed at midnight and quickly returned to the affairs of the kingdom. In the midst of the rubbles and earthquake, Paul preached the gospel to the jailer, and he and his family – and by extension the city – came to the Lord because of it. Hallelujah!

God's strategies work.

It is worth being the ridicule and the source of laughter for many. I do not care much if my enemies are talking, murmuring, mocking, or criticizing me. What is important to me is that I am implementing God's strategies; strategies that will give me the victory and propel me to new levels and dimensions. That is what really matters.

People will always find something to criticize you for, whether you do something to deserve it or not. I prefer to be criticized because I believe God and do what He ordered, than to be in good standing with others. I have learned that if my enemies speak of me, and if my name is in the mouth of the devil, it means that I am hitting them hard; because the enemy does not persecute the dead, rather he sends them flowers.

My Prayer

Lord, I lift this prayer to you asking that my readers receive the instructions and specific strategies you have for them so that they can move to a new level. I pray they can understand the importance of receiving and implementing the instructions and specific strategies you have for them, so they can move to their new level. Help them learn to listen to your voice and distinguish it from other voices. Refine their spiritual ears, so they can put to practice the counsel in this chapter; that they saturate themselves with your Word, and that they may be in communion with your Holy Spirit, and spend frequent quality time with you.

I also pray that in addition to discerning the strategies, they have courage to obey and implement them. I pray they do not fear the path of obedience and be willing to pay the price to realize the strategies, even though at face value they may not make sense. I pray they do not let their enemies and criticism intimidate them. I pray they desire doing your will above saving face and their reputation with others. I pray they are completely convinced that your strategies work. I bless them and declare they will not only receive revelation, as Joshua did to conquer Jericho, but also they will be as obedient as he was. In Christ Jesus, we pray. Amen.

My Prophetic Declaration

- I declare that the Lord has prepared instructions and strategies for me so that I can move to my next level. I declare those strategies will bring results.

- I declare I will invest the time necessary to receive my specific strategies from the Lord. And I refuse to improvise, invent, or copy strategies from others.

- I declare I have spiritual ears to know and distinguish the voice of God.

- I declare I am going to be quiet in order to listen to God's voice and instructions.

- I declare I will value and use all the biblical forms possible to receive the pertinent revelation.

- I declare I will be obedient to the instructions the Lord gives me. I will execute and implement them no matter the price.

- I declare I will pay the price of obedience. I am resolved to implement the strategies God gives me because I am interested in advancing to my new level, and not solely in obtaining the acceptance of others.

- I am willing to do what God asks me to do no matter how ridiculous I look doing it. I am willing to sacrifice my image and reputation.

- I declare I am not afraid of my enemies. I know each attack confirms I am headed in the right direction, because my enemy does not persecute dead people, but rather sends them flowers.

PROMISES

CHAPTER 9

"For all the promises of God in Him are Yes, and in Him Amen, to the glory of God through us."
2nd *Corinthians 1:20*

The next thing we need to consider to advance to a new level is the promises God has for us. The Word of God not only contains commandments, precepts, statues, spiritual laws, orders, and strategies; but it is also filled with hundreds of promises starting from Genesis and on through to Revelation. There are promises for each season and occasion of our lives.

We need the commands of the Lord as well as His promises. In our spiritual walk, we cannot overlook the promises of the Lord. It is worth spending time to know, identify, study, and memorize them; so that we can ultimately claim and activate them in our lives.

The promises of God are there to be claimed.

If you ignore the promises of the Lord, you will not be able to activate them and you will lose their impact in your life. The promises of the Lord are powerful. They are additional resources deposited in your *spiritual reserves* account to be used at the opportune time.

The promises of God serve to push you towards your divine purpose, to help you fulfill your calling, to inspire, encourage, and grant you power. We can see that for each person the Lord called, He also gave them specific promises. There is a direct relationship between their calling and the promises. The promises are not given to you to boast or play with; they are given to you to push you to your calling. In other words, your promises are part of your calling.

Consider Isaiah 42:6-7. The first part of verse 6 talks about a calling and verse 7 talks about the purpose of that calling and the assignment given. But the second part of verse 6 captures the promises:

> "I will hold Your hand; I will keep You and give You as a covenant to the people, as a light to the Gentiles."

The same thing happens with Joshua, the conqueror. Read Joshua 1:2-9, highlighted in part below.

The calling: Joshua 1:2
- "Moses My servant is dead. Now therefore, arise."

The commission: Joshua 1:2-4, 6
- "Go over this Jordan ... Every place that the sole of your foot will tread upon I have given you ... To this people you shall divide as an inheritance the land."

Commands: Joshua 1:6, 9
- "Be strong and of good courage ... do not be afraid, nor be dismayed."

Strategies to overcome: Joshua 1:8
- "This Book of the Law shall not depart from your mouth, but you shall meditate in it day and night, that you may observe to do according to all that is written in it."

Promises to encourage and grant power: Joshua 1:5, 7,-9
- "No man shall be able to stand before you all the days of your life." (v. 5)
- "As I was with Moses, so I will be with you." (v. 5)
- "I will not leave you nor forsake you." (v. 5)
- "You may prosper wherever you go." (v. 7)
- "You will have good success." (v. 8)
- "The LORD your God is with you wherever you go." (v. 9)

Trying to fulfill your calling without taking into account the promises of the Lord is not the same than to be endorsed by the powerful promises of God. There is a great difference. How valuable and important are the promises of the Lord! There is a vast difference between having them and not having them.

There are people who throughout our lives promise us many things. Many do not even have the slightest intention of fulfilling them; others have the best desire of fulfilling them, but lack the capacity and power to do so. Many may keep their promises today, but cannot assure you they will keep them tomorrow, for they do not know if they will be alive then.

> **God does not have a problem fulfilling what he has promised, He is God.**

The Apostle Paul declared in 2nd Corinthians 1:20 that **all** of God's promises, not some but all, "are Yes, and in Him Amen." All of His promises are trustworthy. The writer, in Hebrews 10:23, adds to hold unshakably to the hope we profess because of one powerful reason: "**For He who promised is faithful**." God is faithful. The Word says that clearly He fulfills what He promises; He does not lie. He will do what He said He would do.

> "God is not a man, that He should lie, nor a son of man, that He should repent. Has He said, and will He not do? Or has He spoken, and will He not make it good?"   Numbers 23:19

God does not have any problems with clear-cut words such as: always, never, everyday, all, continually, and eternally. For Him, always is always without any exceptions. What a great guarantee! There is no one who can take over His sovereignty or make Him not fulfill what He promises. That is why He is God.

God told Israel:

> "Fear not, for I am with you; be not dismayed, for I
> am your God. I will strengthen you, yes, I will help
> you, I will uphold you with My righteous right
> hand."   Isaiah 41:10

Jesus, when parting from his disciples, promised He would be with them, not some days or if it was possible; **but every day, until the end of the world.** (Matthew 28:20).

By His inherent capacity, God does not fear that we remind Him and claim His promises. By the way, He allowed them to be written in His book for perpetuity so that you and I would have the opportunity to know, claim, and activate them in our lives.

When a promise of God does not happen in us, we know the problem is not in God. He does not have a problem fulfilling His promises, for He is God at all times. He reigns and is seating in his throne. Therefore, the problem is in us. There is something we have stopped doing or we did something we should not have done; we have probably overlooked something. Let us remember that some promises are unconditional, but others are conditional. If we do our part, God will do His. One thing I am certain of, all of God's promises work. There are hundreds and hundreds of promises the Lord has given us to cover each need, condition, or season of our lives.

In each one of the great promises the Lord gives to Joshua, we observe three groupings:

- **Promises of Prosperity** – guarantees to have all the necessary resources to be able to fulfill our purpose.

- **Promises of Protection** – guarantees to receive the protection of the Lord, in such a way so we can fulfill what He has given us, despite of the enemies that may rise up.

- **Promises of Presence** – guarantees that we can count with His unconditional presence, so we can fulfill what we have been assigned regardless of where we go or how difficult a task we face.

Let us examine each category of God's promises to Joshua.

1) Promise of Prosperity.

The Lord tells Joshua that when he undertakes what He has commanded him to do, He will prosper him (Joshua 1:7). To prosper here means: I am personally going to take care of everything that is needed so you will have all the resources, whether spiritual, physical, or material, so you can finish what you have undertaken. Nehemiah had the same revelation, which he boldly told his enemy Sanballat to his face. Sanballat was questioning the calling, capacity, and the resources needed by Nehemiah and the people to restore the city. But Nehemiah answers him and clarifies all doubt:

> "The God of heaven Himself will prosper us; therefore we His servants will arise and build ..."
> Nehemiah 2:20

Nehemiah was certain he could successfully accomplish what God had asked him to do, for the same God who called him was going to prosper him, and would give him everything necessary in due time. Hallelujah! Our source of provision is God. There is a very good reason his name is Yahweh Yireh – the God who provides. "The silver is mine, and the gold is mine" (Haggai 2:8); "the earth is the Lord's and everything in it, the world and all who live in it" (Psalm 24:1). Truthfully, "God shall supply all your need according to His riches in glory by Christ Jesus" (Philippians 4:19).

God is interested in prospering our path, in our success, in seeing us fulfill our mission, and advance to a new level.

God does not promote failure or defeat. Do not be afraid of being prospered by God. True prosperity is from God, not from the devil.

We need to activate the prosperity of God so that it propels us towards our calling, our ministries, to be able to advance in faith. Psalm 35:27 (AMP) declares that God is delighted with our wellbeing, and our prosperity.

> "Shout for joy and be glad and say continually, Let the Lord be magnified, who takes pleasure in the prosperity of His servant."

Let us remember he is Yahweh Shalom. The word Shalom addresses the whole well-being of a person: physical, emotional, spiritual, and material. It is an integral well-being equipping us to do the will of God. It is very difficult for a sick person, someone who is captive, emotionally unbalanced, in sin, misery, poverty, or scarcity and without resources, to fulfill his purpose in life at the required time and with the demanded quality. Prosperity does not come from the devil, like many people think. If that were the case, then Nehemiah's declaration would be anti-biblical. Prosperity is not from the devil, otherwise the desire of the beloved and wise Apostle John to his sons would be a sin:

> "Beloved I pray that **in all respects you may prosper** and be in good health, just as your soul prospers."
>
> 3rd John 2

Prosperity cannot be from the devil; if it was, then the promise of prosperity Joshua received could not have been from God. Nevertheless, the God who told him that He would be with him and defend him was the same God who told him He would prosper him.

Many Christians do not have a problem with the promise of protection and the promise of presence; however, they do have a problem with the promise of prosperity. All three are necessary and all three come from the same source, God.

Throughout my personal, familial, and ministerial life, I have experienced divine provision. I have seen how God has released necessary resources, on time, to carry out God's agenda. In the most difficult times, we have seen how God has sent his crows with provision: food, clothes, money, company, intercessors, a hug, a prophetic word, or a word of encouragement.

I remember when we were co-pastors in our mother church in Puerto Rico, God asked me to resign from my secular job as a music teacher. My wife and I entered into a stage of pure faith, believing the Lord would give us everything necessary, and would not leave us in shame. It was a time of living in expectation, day-by-day and minute-by-minute.

One Friday night while we were both doing the dishes, we were praying together and we asked the Lord for two specific things. The first thing was that we wanted to change the menu. For almost an entire week, we had been eating hot dogs that we bought at a very low price. My wife had already exhausted every possibility, cooking them in many different ways. That Friday we wanted to eat chicken, and more specifically, Kentucky Fried Chicken. The only problem we had was that we did not have money. But we prayed and asked the Lord.

The second thing we prayed for was for the Lord to provide us with $100 to be able to pay some pending bills. We prayed specifically, we thanked him, and went to the Friday night service.

When the service finished, I went to the door to greet the brethren. The first to come to the door were part of the youth group and were our friends. They greeted us saying: "Pastors, we would like to invite you to eat chicken at KFC, is that alright with you?" You already know the answer to that! More from the church continued passing by and then a sister approached me to say hello and at the same time she quickly puts an envelope in my hand. I put it in my shirt pocket, thinking that it was a prayer petition, a common practice. When my wife and I were on our way to eat dinner, I remembered the envelope, opened it and there was in it a folded $100 bill. We gave glory to God, and confirmed once more that God is our provider.

We thanked the sister the following Sunday and she told me that she had received some money from an inheritance and had decided to set some of it aside for me. The amount she first had in mind was $25, so she took the money and put it in an envelope. After a few minutes, she did not feel at peace and she understood the Lord was telling her she needed to give more. After a few long minutes, she switched the $25 for a $100 bill. Then, she swapped the $100 for the $25 and she continued doing so many times, until she finally left the $100 bill. I explained to her the reason for her switching the bills: my wife and I had prayed for a $100, not $25, and God used her to answer our prayer. She opened her eyes wide; she could not believe the decision of switching the bills was not hers, but an order the Lord had given her. Hallelujah! The Lord provides.

On another occasion, the engine of my relatively new car had stopped working. Various mechanics came to see the car and confirmed the diagnosis. Nevertheless, none of the mechanics fixed it, because I did not have the money to pay for the labor or the engine. My wife and I, along with another brother, prayed during that week for God to intervene. We asked God to either fix the car or provide the money to fix it. After a week, a church member with a tow truck came to take it to the mechanic. He had talked to the mechanic so that we can pay for it in installments. The person who came over told me: "Pastor, turn on the car so we hear how it sounds." So I did it, waiting to hear that evil sound of the engine, but instead the car turned on softly, without any noise. We got in the car and went on the road, driving it long enough to realize God had made provision, a miracle; He had fixed our car. Hallelujah! What a testimony! I can go on for a while testifying about how God has prospered us, but let me share only two more.

I was in the beautiful country of Chile, on a missionary trip with a musical group I directed. We went by faith to that country, for no one knew us or expected us. The day we arrived, God spoke to a pastor telling him to go to his pastoral supervisor's office. He found us there. When he found out who we were and what we were there for, he took us to his church, looked after our transportation and lodging, housing us with brethren from the church, and organized a tour for the two weeks we were there. We prayed under the cloudless sky of Chile's airport around nine o'clock at night, with no connections or support, asking the Lord to bring the right pastor, and He did. Hallelujah!

When we got to the airport to leave Chile, we weighed the luggage and it turned out it weighed too much. We had the music and sound equipment and our own luggage. The cost to bring on the excess weight was about $500 and we only had $200; not a dollar more. If we did not pay in full, the luggage could not go. In the midst of that uncertainty and negotiation, we prayed to the Lord. Suddenly, out of the office comes an employee who appeared to have some kind of authority for the airline, seemed unaware of what was going on, and tells the person who is dealing with us to process the luggage weight using a certain computation. The check-in agent obeys, redoes the numbers and tells me: "now it is $200." Hallelujah! As for me, I am sure that an angel from the Lord came to our help through the mystery employee, who came out of nowhere to help and then disappeared. God provides.

I could also tell you how God provided for the down payment of our new house. How I prayed each day on my treadmill, for the twenty thousand that were left for the down payment. It was amazing to see, how in three and a half months, I miraculously received that amount. People who brought me money knew neither about my prayer request nor the amount needed. It is one thing for someone to give you $500 and perhaps another $100, but $20,000! That is certainly uncommon. Some people gave us $500, some gave us $1,000, others $2,500, and someone gave us $7,000. Simply put, this is the prosperity and provision of God. I believe it, receive it, and preach it; do you?

Activate today your promise for divine provision. Can you believe God is powerful to supply the need you are experiencing right now? Do you think God is capable of providing the money and resources you need? Can you trust God to help you make the right contacts, get the job or better position you seek, or be given a salary increase or promotion? Do you think God is capable of giving you grace and favor? Do you believe the will of God for you is to prosper in all things? If the answer to these questions is yes, then activate your promise of prosperity and say as Nehemiah did: The God of Heaven will prosper me. Say as the Psalmist did: God is pleased when I am well. Hallelujah!

2) Promise of Protection

God tells Joshua, when he goes to the Promised Land, towards his new level: "No one will come against you." In other words, he was told no one enemy would be able to defeat him because Jehovah was with him. It is necessary to remind you that on your way towards your new level and calling there are many enemies who every now and then will cross your path with the purpose of detaining you, making you turn back, or taking you off course. When the Lord gives this promise of protection to Joshua, it was because he would need it.

You also have enemies who have as their assignment blocking your path and seeing to it that you are defeated. They are not playing games with you; they want to rob you of your dreams, your visions, your blessings, and your promotion. The attack is virulent, constant, and powerful. Paul advices us with certainty not to ignore the schemes of the enemy (2nd Corinthians 2:11). This is why God has given you promises of protection, but it is necessary that you activate them each day.

You cannot risk living exposed, vulnerable and walking about unprotected.

There are promises of protection that you should claim constantly. Let us look at some examples of them.

> "No weapon formed against you shall prosper, and every tongue which rises against you in judgment you shall condemn. This is the heritage of the servants of the LORD, and their righteousness is from Me, says the LORD." Isaiah 54:17

Ephesians 6:16 says God has given us the shield of faith so you can extinguish all the flaming arrows of the evil one. Furthermore, David declared that God himself was his shield around him. His adversaries had multiplied, but David was safe because he had a great shield (Psalm 3:1-3). Jabez knew when he began to expand his territory, he had to face evil. This is why he prayed to God and said: keep me from harm (1st Chronicles 4:10). Jabez knew God not only had the capacity to bless him, but also, the ability to protect him.

We cannot prevent weapons from forming or tongues from rising up against us. We cannot keep the enemy from throwing his arrows of flames or from multiplying, but listen to this:

When you activate the promises of protection, the weapons of the enemy will not prosper; we will be able to condemn every tongue, turn off the darts of fire, declare that God is our shield, and be kept from harm.

Our Protector is the Lion of the tribe of Judah, **Jesus**, the One who has not lost a battle, the One who conquered sin, sickness, strongholds, the world, death itself, and the One who stepped on the devil's head.

A while back, I heard a story of a wolf who found a baby bear that had been separated from its mother bear. "What a great banquet!" the wolf said. The baby bear prepared for the worst. He was waiting for the wolf to jump on him and devour him, but suddenly he sees the wolf opens his eyes with an expression of terror; and then proceed to turn his back to the baby bear and run away. In awe of what was happening, the baby bear looks back and sees his mother standing on two feet in an attack position. This made the wolf run away; mother bear was protecting her cub. In the same manner, **Jesus is in an attack position for his children protecting us and so no one will be able to rise against us.**

God was telling Joshua in that promise (Joshua 1:5): I am your protector; I am larger than any enemy that may come against you. David also experienced this truth in Psalm 138:7.

"Though I walk in the midst of trouble, You will revive me; You will stretch out Your hand against the wrath of my enemies, and Your right hand will save me."

When the enemy believes we have been abandoned or we are dying, and comes with the final attack, he is surprised by our resurrection. The Lord revives us and gives us a second wind – a new opportunity. The enemies will see how the right hand of God saves us and how with His other hand He takes care of His children. Hallelujah!

I often travel to different countries to supervise and minister to the churches in our network. I have been to places like Iquitos and Nauta, Peruvian cities in the Amazon. I have also been to different cities in Honduras, Dominican Republic, Cuba, Argentina, Puerto Rico, and Spain.

We have been in faraway places, we have been through some dangerous routes, with vehicles in bad conditions, lodging in dangerous places that were not too hygienic, having to eat or drink things that could make our bodies sick, and facing bad weather while in flight; but through it all God has protected and guarded us. I know angels have been busy, ministering protection during those times. Hallelujah! The Lord has given us His grace, His health, and protection.

I ask you now: Do you believe that God is your protector? Do you desire to activate that promise in your life today? Do you believe that God is greater than any situation you are facing? Do you believe that God is greater than that sickness, that problem with your children, that financial burden, that situation on your job, or that personal relationship that has deteriorated? Do you believe God is greater than all those people who have taken the task of criticizing and harming you or than those doors that have all of the sudden closed for no apparent reason? Do you believe the one who is with you is greater and that nothing can stand against you? Do you truly believe it? Then, activate your promise of protection;

do not fear, but trust in the Lord. Can you pray right now, and declare prophetically in your favor part of Psalm 91?

> "My God, in Him I will trust. Surely He shall deliver you from the snare of the fowler and from the perilous pestilence. He shall cover you with His feathers, and under His wings you shall take refuge; His truth shall be your shield and buckler. You shall not be afraid of the terror by night, nor of the arrow that flies by day, nor of the pestilence that walks in darkness, nor of the destruction that lays waste at noonday. A thousand may fall at your side, and ten thousand at your right hand; but it shall not come near you. Only with your eyes shall you look, and see the reward of the wicked. Because you have made the LORD, who is my refuge, even the Most High, your dwelling place, no evil shall befall you, nor shall any plague come near your dwelling; for He shall give His angels charge over you, to keep you in all your ways."

3) Promise of his Presence

The Lord's third promise for Joshua was the certainty of His presence, regardless of where Joshua had to go in obedience to His calling and vision. God would be with Joshua. There are places you might have to step on and no one else can accompany you. In fact, there will be laws or norms that will prohibit anyone to go with you.

Every place is within the Lord's reach. No one can prevent Him from being where He wants. No one can prevent God from manifesting His power and grace.

Obviously, the schedule for visitors in jails or in hospitals does not apply to Jesus. Nor would a sign of "Authorized Personnel Only" deter Him when a patient is taken to the operating room; there Jesus is. In the midst of a trip to dangerous places, there Jesus goes. When we have to attend meetings or events with important people, where attendance is selective; if we have to be there, the Lord will be with us.

Even though Peter was incarcerated and well guarded by soldiers, the angel of the Lord did not have any problems going into the cell, waking up Peter from his sleep, delivering him from his chains, and guarding him until they got outside. In spite of the efforts and the security measures that Herod took, the angel of the Lord went inside the jail cell and delivered Peter (Acts 12:6-11).

Even though Daniel was thrown into the lion's den and trapped with security, the angel of the Lord did not have any problem going in to accompany the prophet, and above all, close the mouths of the lions (Daniel 6).

Even though there were three young Hebrews who were thrown into the oven of fire, the king himself gave testimony of a fourth man who was walking freely among the youth, and his image was like the son of the gods. Certainly, the angel of the Lord did not have any problems accompanying these faithful young men nor delivering them from the oven of fire, despite the efforts of the king to burn them alive (Daniel 3).

When the boat where the Apostle Paul was incarcerated encountered a great storm, Paul was able to testify to the rest of the crew, that the angel of the Lord whom he served had been there that night and had shared with him what was going to happen. Paul told them to take heart, because even if the boat shipwrecked, there would not be any lives lost (Acts 27:21-24) Hallelujah!

> **There is no jail, den, oven of fire, or storm in the deep sea that would prevent the presence and protection of the Lord.**

David declared that he could be still, at peace, and without fear even in the valley of the shadow of death, because the Lord (the pastor) was with him (Psalm 23:4). When we know the Lord is there, faith grows in us, trust, courage, strength, and the desire to continue forward and cross whatever we need to cross. If He is there, He will not abandon us: "I will not leave you or forsake you" (Joshua 1:5b), therefore He will work to our favor.

This promise has sustained me throughout my ministerial life. It is in the most difficult and darkest times when you least *feel* the presence of the Lord. In these situations, we tend to reach quick conclusions. Immediately we conclude we are by ourselves, that God has forgotten us because we do not *feel* God. Nevertheless, the promise of presence is the one that makes me come to my senses. This promise does not say I have to feel or see Him. God's promises have nothing to do with my natural senses or with my emotions. The Lord promises He will be there always, whether I feel Him or not, HE IS THERE. As long as I do His will, He will be there. The promise releases faith in me and the faith that is released makes me believe in His promise even more. One feeds the other. The promise of His presence is key for the rest of the promises. What good is it to have money, resources, strength, intelligence, friends, health, and positions, if you lack His presence?

> **Having Him is the most important thing, because when you have Him you have everything: provision, health, strength, resources, grace, protection, and victory.**

Remember that if Jehovah is our pastor, then, we shall not want (Psalm 23:1).

My Prayer

Heavenly Father I ask you that my dear readers can understand the importance of knowing and claiming each promise you have left for their benefit. I pray each time they claim any of your promises that they may advance towards their new level and fulfill their purpose in life. That they can trust you completely, knowing you are faithful to fulfill everything you have promised.

I pray they can claim and activate the promises of prosperity in your Word. That they can release all the necessary resources at the proper time. That they may be like a Nehemiah of this time, who knows where their provision will come from, and that you will prosper them. Let them be convinced you created them to have success and victory, not to fail, and stay half way on the path. Thank you Lord, because you will supply everything they will need.

I pray they can claim and activate the promises of protection throughout their journey. That they may never go forward lacking anything or without your protection. That like Joshua, they can be confident no one will be able to stand against them, because you are their shield and no weapon forged against them will prosper. We rebuke all fear and declare the victory of the Lord over their enemies.

I pray they can claim and activate the promises of your presence. That they may understand they are never alone; that there is no place where the obedience to your calling will take them that you are not be able to be with them. That like Joshua, they may have the conviction in their spirits that you will go with them wherever they go. That they may declare with certainty: you are God in every place and at all times. In Christ Jesus, we pray. Amen.

My Prophetic Declaration

- I declare I will walk towards my new level supported in all of God's promises for me. My divine calling is supported by God's promises.

- I declare the promises of God will propel me to my new level and will open the way to my victory.

- I declare God is powerful and faithful to fulfill what He has promised. God is not of man that He should lie; what He says, He will fulfill.

- I declare that I will activate God's promises of prosperity. I will not lack anything to execute the plans of God. He is the source of my resources, He is Yahweh Yireh.

- I declare that I will activate God's promises of protection. I will not fear any harm, for God is my shield. If God is for me, who can be against me. God is greater than any enemy.

- I declare that I will activate God's promises of presence. I walk in confidence, for I know that He is with me wherever I go. He is my shadow at my right hand. He will not forsake me, nor leave. If I have Him, I have everything. Amen.

GOOD STEWARDSHIP

CHAPTER 10

"As each one has received a gift, minister it to one another, as good stewards of the manifold grace of God."   *1st Peter 4:10*

A nother requirement necessary to reach your new level is to be a good steward of everything you have. Those who are living in disorder, chaos, anarchy, and disorganization cannot advance to new levels. Lack of organization provokes delays. There is a direct relationship between good stewardship and advancement, promotion, and success.

> **Your calling, divine purpose, vision, and advancement to the new level are supported by your ability to be a good steward.**

What do we understand by stewardship? It is the process of identifying all the available resources and our ability to use them in an efficient way to reach our goals and complete our projects. In this sense, we are all called to be stewards in life. We have all received resources, spiritual gifts, and God's blessings along with specific callings (James 1:17). Of course, the challenge goes beyond being stewards. The challenge is to be good stewards according to 1st Peter 4:10b.

"As each one... as good stewards of the manifold grace of God."

In order to be good stewards we first need to know what our purpose and calling in life is, where we are going, and why. In other words, we need to discern the vision for our lives. Then we should identify all the resources available to us.

Some already know what their calling is and have a vision. Their problem consists in that they have not identified all of their resources. You cannot use or maximize what you do not know you have. To have resources available and not use them or ignore them is bad stewardship.

Hagar, Sarah's servant, almost died in the desert with her child. The sad thing was she was dying of thirst and exhaustion right next to an oasis, next to a water well. The passage shows us that the real miracle from God was not the creation and provision of the water well, but rather that Hagar's eyes were opened so she could see that what she needed was right next to her.

> "And the water in the skin was used up, and she placed the boy under one of the shrubs. Then she went and sat down across from *him* at a distance of about a bowshot; for she said to herself, Let me not see the death of the boy... Then God opened her eyes, and she saw a well of water. And she went and filled the skin with water, and gave the lad a drink."
>
> Genesis 21:15-16, 19

In this situation, we can observe Hagar did not make an inventory of her resources. She was not able to see what she should have seen and almost died because of it. Many today are crying and lamenting their situation next to their oasis. They think just like Hagar, who thought the only resource to sustain her was the house of Abraham and did not know or appreciate that God has many resources available at our disposal. Being spiritually blind is worse than being physically blind. To fulfill your destiny you need to see everything you are and everything you already have from God. Good stewardship demands that you do a spiritual inventory day after day.

It is foolish to ask the Lord to give us more things, if we have not even invested the time to discover and use what we already have.

When the disciples told Jesus that the multitude was dying of hunger, and that it was late in the day, Jesus said: examine more closely the true state of the multitude and verify what is available; go and see (Mark 6:38). It was after that order that Andrew brought the boy with the basket which Jesus used to multiply and feed the multitude. There was a lesson of stewardship in that order: **If we have not used everything God has given us, why ask for more.** Let us begin by using what we already have.

In the same manner, after feeding the multitude and having appeased their hunger, the writer says that 12 full baskets of leftovers were collected. Jesus gave the order to collect the leftovers and for nothing to go to waste (John 6:12-13). Here is another lesson of good stewardship. **Jesus does not sponsor wastefulness or the wrong use of blessings.**

I hear many testify about their dreams, visions, and callings, time after time; but I see little progress is made in the area of stewardship of their possessions. I hear their visions, but at the same time, I see the disaster and lack of stewardship in which they live. They cannot see the correlation that exists between excellent stewardship and the realization of their dreams; between excellent stewardship and the progression to new levels.

> **Visions and callings need to be operated under good stewardship.**

Everyone who lacks structure, order, and organization, will condemn himself or herself to being where they have always been. Sadly, on their way to progress, these people will see others who began after them pass them by. Their business will go bankrupt, their ministries will not progress, their finances will be stuck, and all because of deficiencies in the area of stewardship.

Now is the time to place all things in God's order, no matter which level you find yourself in. It is your time to improve your system of stewardship, to acquire the knowledge you need, establish and lift up the necessary structures and discipline, and learn how to maximize the finite resource of time. You must organize yourself.

It is crucial to remember that our God is a God of order. God does not honor confusion and lack of organization (1st Corinthians 14:32). The first two verses of Psalm 133 give us a model of how the order of the Lord frees our promotion and blessing. Order is more important than what we might think.

> "Behold, how good and how pleasant *it is* for brethren to dwell together in unity! *It is* like the precious oil upon the head, running down on the beard, the beard of Aaron, running down on the edge of his garments."

The Psalm says the anointing begins to flow from the head (of the Lord), and later through the beard (of Aaron), and descends all the way down to the edge of the clothes. The anointing has an order. The beard cannot operate above the head, or the clothes above the beard. The head cannot be relegated to the clothes. Everything must be in its place, in the appropriate order, and corresponding succession.

Similarly, we see the same process in the construction of the tabernacle by Moses. Before the glory of the Lord could be manifested, there had to be an order. God gave detailed instructions to Moses about the way the tabernacle was to be constructed. In a very clear way, God spoke to Moses about all aspects of the construction and who should serve in it. Once they followed the established divine order, the glory of the Lord was manifested. (29)

Do you know why many do not progress in their faith? Do you know why the anointing does not touch them even though it is God's will for them? It does not because their lives do not align with the order of the Lord. Even if they prayed and fasted asking for anointing, their bad stewardship and lack of order has limited them. People with divine callings are stagnated, stuck, or are producing below their potential because they are out of the order of the Lord. Some are not in the right place, have left or have jumped positions, or have jumped processes and stages. They have not submitted to God's order, wanting to establish their own order.

It is dangerous when people minister who are out of order or out of place, because that is what they will minister unto others. People who are out of order will justify the lack of order and will promote it as something good, condemning those who are with them. When you associate with people who lack order in their lives, that lack of order will also affect you and will delay your steps towards your new level.

In the passage of the feeding of the multitude with the bread and fish, Jesus, before performing the miracle, organized the multitude in groups of 50. It was not until the entire multitude was organized in the way Jesus specified, that the miracle was manifested (Luke 9:14-16).

> **Your miracle is in God's agenda, but it is delayed waiting for you; waiting for you to get organized and flow with God's order.**

I can imagine certain types of people, people who are part of almost every church, being part of that multitude and asking Peter: why do I have to sit down with forty-nine other people? I am not tired and I am not going to sit down. Why in groups of fifty and not twenty-five? They would ask Peter: why have you paired me with these people? I want to be with that group. May be they said: I am a friend of Jesus and I do not think I have to sit down like everyone else. Tell Jesus to exempt me from the groups of fifty and having to wait, because I am too sick and need for him to excuse me from the process and give me priority over the rest.

Do you know people like this; people that find ways not to submit, not follow instructions, and do things their own way. It is challenging for such people to follow an established order and instructions. It is difficult for them to be organized; instead, they flow with the lack of organization and the chaos. I also think there are spiritual bondages that keep people from moving in order and submission. For me, many of them are under rebellious spirits, that they cannot simply resist God's order. Even if they do not have a valid reason to oppose, they still do.

Let us remember the principle under which the enemy operates is the lack of order and disobedience, but the principle under which Jesus operates is submission, obedience, and order. Why is it that many people cannot move to a new level in their finances? They cannot because to do so, order and good administration of their finances is necessary. The reason why there is not enough money in our lives is not always the high cost of living but because of the disastrous ways we manage our finances. We keep asking God for more and more, instead of asking for wisdom to administer better what we do have. It is akin to asking for money because we keep losing what we have instead of sewing our pockets so as not to lose any more money.

Notice how in the parable of the talents, the Lord uses the ability of each servant as criteria to determine how many talents to give them.

> "And to one he gave five talents, to another two, and
> to another one, to each according to his own ability;
> and immediately he went on a journey."
>   Matthew 25:15

This means that if you improve and expand your administrative abilities, the amount trusted to you will be automatically increased. The one who has less is not necessarily given more, but rather more is given to the one who has a better ability to maximize it. This breaks the paradigm and parameters under which we have been operating. We have believed that our abilities and deficiencies are the reason why the Lord provides to us. But we can see in this passage that what releases greater provision from the heavens is our ability to manage effectively what we already have, whether it is little or much. That is why the talent was taken away from the servant who had one, because he was not administrating it well. This one the lord left without anything. However, the one who was given five talents, because of his good administration, saw his talents doubled to ten and furthermore the lord also gave him the talent of the ineffective servant.

> **If you increase your ability to administer, you will increase your ability to receive.**

I am fully convinced we need better stewardship and order in our homes. There are homes that look like they have been abandoned. The houses are messy, dirty, needing a coat of paint, with garbage everywhere, dishes not being done, the lawn not done, and make no mention of the condition of the car. There is no time to clean or straighten the house, but there is time to watch three hours of television. Why would people who do not take care of their possessions want more?

The majority of what I describe above is learned behavior. Many have received an inheritance of informality, improvisation, neglect, irresponsibility, and mediocrity from their previous generation and even from their cultural inheritance. Attitudes such as: "so what? It is what it is, that is not my problem, I do not care if I am late" show our philosophy regarding stewardship.

We need to be free from that inheritance that does not allow us to progress; we must be free from all negative habits that do not allow us to advance. The search for such freedom and the preservation of it are the necessary steps to be good stewards.

I was impacted by the way Pastor Weeks explains in his book, Even As Your Soul Prospers, the mandatory stop God orders Moses to do while he and the people of God were on their way to the Promised Land (Exodus 19). Pastor Weeks says that it was necessary to stop between the exodus and the arrival to the Promised Land. Remember the people were slaves for many years. Now they were going to enter an environment of freedom as a nation. They needed order, structure, and laws, in order to function in their new level.[30] That is why, when the people arrive at Mount Sinai, God stops. There He begins to give them laws regarding worship, ceremonies, sacrifices, hygiene, and civil laws. These instructions were given primarily in the book of Leviticus.

In order for the people to enter their new level, they first had to be taken out of Egypt, and from their slavery condition. This is the exodus. Without an exodus in our lives, we cannot extend ourselves to the new things God has in store for us. Slaves, and those of a slave mentality, cannot expand their horizons; they cannot grow or move to new levels. On the other hand, it is not enough to leave the negative environment. Before entering a new level, God stopped the people at Mount Sinai and gave them structure, laws, and order for them to function victoriously in their new level (Leviticus). This is how Pastor Weeks says it:

> "So it was necessary for Israel to stop at Sinai because they had to regroup – *set things in order* – before moving forward into their destiny ... reclaiming and possessing the Promised Land."[31]

It is not enough to leave Egypt and reach the Promised Land; you need a Leviticus in your life. You need structure, order, principles, and laws. You need to have good stewardship before ascending and arriving at your new level. Your Promised Land demands for you to have good stewardship.

It is dangerous to step into your new level without good stewardship. The challenge it is not just to arrive but also to remain in that victory.

Many of those who are reading this book already left Egypt and are free in Christ; but they are delayed in Sinai, because God is working with them and getting them to be good stewards of what they have and are about to receive. There is no problem with this mandatory delay, every time we go towards a new level, there will be an Exodus and a Leviticus. However, problems come for those who resist this stop, for those who are not learning, or who are wasting time, and for those who do not see the reason they need to be in Sinai and reject the principles of good stewardship insisting on doing things their own way.

I have news for you: forget about the new level, you will remain in Sinai day after day, year after year, until you pass the *course* on good stewardship. The time of your stay in Sinai will depend on you. When you learn what you have to learn, God will move you to the new level. If you resist or you pay little attention to this process, you will extend your time at Sinai.

God is eternal, He does not have a problem with time, but we do. Time goes by quickly and there are opportunities that only present themselves once in a lifetime.

> **If you extend your time in Sinai, you will be reducing your time in the Promised Land.**

Maximizing your stop to equip and prepare is not wasted time. Such pause is necessary to advance, to establish oneself, and have victory in the new level. Set as a goal today to be a good steward of all God has put on your hands. Seek whatever spiritual and professional help is necessary to improve your administrative aptitude. If you follow this advice, it will not weigh you down or hold you back, but rather you will see how certain areas of your life will begin to flourish, bear fruit, and produce positive results that will propel you to your new level.

Chapter 10 Notes

(29) <u>Walk in God's Pattern for Success</u> - John Bevere - Charisma House 2002 (p. 14-15)

(30) <u>Even As Your Soul Prospers</u> - Thomas Weeks III - Harrison House 2004 (p. 59-61)

(31) <u>Even As Your Soul Prospers</u> - Thomas Weeks III - Harrison House 2004 (p. 61)

My Prayer

Lord, we desire to be good stewards according to your word. Remove from my readers all resistance to improve their stewardship abilities. Create a conscience of understanding the importance of good stewardship.

I pray also for a clear vision, calling, and purpose. I pray so they may make an inventory of their life and discover all the things that are available for them. I pray they make good use of all the resources you have made available at their disposal.

I pray so they may overcome any family or cultural inheritance of bad habits in the management of possessions, time, and resources. I rebuke all spirit of rebellion, lack of order that they may be trapped in and impede their advancement. I declare them free to appreciate order, beauty, and organization. That they may flow with the structures God has given them. I pray so they may not be trapped between the Exodus and Sinai for the rest of their lives, but that they may be able to move to a new level. In Christ Jesus, we pray. Amen.

My Prophetic Declaration

- I declare I will be a good steward of all the resources God has given me and will give me.

- I declare I will make an inventory of my life in order to know all the resources, gifts, abilities, and blessings God has given me to use in the advancement of God's calling in my life.

- I declare I will renew my mind so I may appreciate and value the importance and worth of good stewardship.

- I declare that I renounce the negative habits that have been in my ancestors for many years and are now in my family. I renounce cultural customs and traditions I have received as part of my inheritance and that only have delayed my calling.

- I declare I value my Sinai, my stop in the journey. I will maximize my time in this school of the Lord each time I may be in it, because I am determined to reach my new level and remain in Him. I refuse to remain all my life in Sinai because of my lack of cooperation and learning.

- I declare I flow with God's order, structure, and organization and I let go of every spirit of rebellion and disorder in my life. I declare myself free in Christ. I advance in faith supported by the principles of Christ and not by the principles of the enemy.

FAITHFULNESS
CHAPTER 11

"... You were faithful over a few things, I will make you ruler over many things ..."

Matthew 25:21

To move to a new level, we need to learn to be faithful in the level that we are in. Every promotion should take into account the level of faithfulness and loyalty of all those who desire to climb higher. It is not just a question of talent, charisma, or intelligence; it is also a matter of faithfulness.

It is dangerous to promote unfaithful people.

It makes no sense to promote people who have not done a good work with what they have been entrusted. The biblical principle Jesus taught says:

"You were faithful over a few things, I will make you ruler over many things..." Matthew 25:21

"He who is faithful in what is least is faithful also in much." Luke 16:10

If you cannot manage well the "few things," how can you ask the Lord to promote you? If you are careless, lazy, and irresponsible, how can others believe that you are ready for new levels? Who will promote you? Your time in the "few things" is more important than you imagine. Many despise and devalue the time in the "few things," the time in anonymity, the time of hiding, the time when one is invisible to others. Many do not see the benefit or any reason for that time in their lives; they are so impatient while waiting for their promotion they neglect their level of the "few things."

Some are upset because time after time they are still the Timothy and not Paul, Elisha and not Elijah, Joshua and not Moses. They ask themselves: until when will I be behind the scenes and serving others? But part of the reason for your season in the few things is for you to learn to be faithful in the few things.

> **If you learn to be faithful in the few things, sooner or later your promotion or advancement will come.**

Focus on being faithful. Concern yourself with doing well those things that have been delegated to you, with excellence and joy. If you are the deacon of the parking lot, be faithful; if you are the assistant to the teacher in the nursery, be faithful; if you are the person serving food in the Open Pantry, be faithful; if you are an assistant pastor, be faithful.

> **To rise to your next level, you do not need to make yourself noticeable; rather your good work and your faithfulness will speak for you.**

To release your promotion and advancement, you do not need to destroy the person who is over you or in charge of you. You do not need to criticize them, speak badly about them, make trouble with others, point out their faults, or betray them. Be careful of not falling into schemes, conflict, envies, and power struggles. Stop questioning why someone else was promoted and you were not. Stop saying that your boss or even the Lord was mistaken and that you were the right person to be promoted. That kind of behavior and attitude reveal on their own that you are not ready to be promoted to your new level; your heart and your tongue are contaminated and have roots of rebellion.

Can you rejoice with the success, recognition, and promotion others receive or does it bother you? If you cannot rejoice with the blessings of others, do not expect others to rejoice when your promotion comes. Do not get upset then, when others question your advancement. My advice to you is that you stop looking and evaluating others and rather concern yourself with your own person, and the work you have been entrusted with, and to do so faithfully. Your time in the few things and in anonymity is there to help you refine your administrative abilities, character, and integrity. Take good advantage of that time!

Note the season of the few things for King David. He was the youngest of his brothers and he spent the majority of his time taking care of his father's flocks. He spent many vigils in the night alone with his sheep. Nobody counted on him; he went unnoticed by almost everyone. In fact, when the Prophet Samuel went to the house of his father to anoint the next king of Israel, he asks Jesse to bring together all of his sons. Jesse calls all of his sons, yet David was excluded. They left him taking care of the sheep. When God tells Samuel none of those first assembled would be the anointed, Samuel asks Jesse if he has any other sons. It is then they remember David and send for him. Certainly it was a time when David was invisible to men, but not to God. The Lord had seen how David had been faithful in the few things and that he had a heart towards Him. David was anointed and selected to be the king of Israel. Never despise your time in the few things.

David knew how to maximize his time in anonymity; he made it work in his favor. Not only was he a good shepherd, but he also learned to kill lions and bears. Those abilities prepared him for his next level: killing giants. In his time of anonymity, he learned to handle his sling, rod, and staff. He learned to play the harp, compose psalms, and above all to have an intimate communion with God.

Every test of faithfulness requires time.

The Lord wants us to demonstrate that we are faithful in the few things before promoting us to the level of the many things.   Anyone can be faithful for two days, but not necessarily for five years.   Every test of fidelity requires time. All spouses can be faithful in their honeymoon; the challenge is being faithful after five, ten, twenty years, or until death. Consider the case of Elisha.   With great joy, he left what he was doing to follow the Prophet Elijah after he had thrown his mantle on him.   The act symbolized that Elisha had been selected to substitute the man of God in his prophetic ministry. It reads this way in 1st King 19:21:

> "Then he arose and followed Elijah, and became his
> servant."

Do you know how much time Elisha spent following Elijah, serving him? Some twenty-five years. He spent all that time following the man of God as a servant. Not as a peer, not as a prophetic collaborator, but rather as a son to a father, as a servant to his or her Lord.

Nowadays many would not have borne out all that time. Perhaps they might bear a couple of years; but after that, it is likely they would have called Elijah aside and told him: "What's going on here? I think my time has now come. Either you pass on the baton or I start my own ministry. I am ready; I know as much as you do."

Anyone can be behind the scenes and serve, if the time is short. The challenge is to wait the necessary time doing what you are told, in a faithful and integral way. It is there where the heart of a faithful and loyal person is revealed.

Paul did not fear or hesitate in recommending, sending, and giving testimony of Timothy to the church in Philippi. He told them he had no one else like him, no one of so kindred a spirit and like-mindedness. He told them Timothy had served as a son, and since Paul could not go to Philippi at that time, sending Timothy was almost as if he would go himself. Paul saw the testimony of Timothy's fidelity in the few things, and now it was his time in the many things.

> "But I trust in the Lord Jesus to send Timothy to you shortly, that I also may be encouraged when I know your state. For I have no one like-minded, who will sincerely care for your state. For all seek their own, not the things which are of Christ Jesus. But you know his proven character, that as a son with his father he served with me in the gospel."
>
> Philippians 2:19-22

Timothy was entrusted at that point in time in the many things; he represented the apostle in a church that was very significant for Paul. The decision to send Timothy was based in his conduct during the time of the few things. Timothy spent a lot of time after Paul, learning, watching, receiving instructions, and serving. Take note of the biblical evidence.

- "Therefore I remind you to stir up the gift of God which is in you through the laying on of **my hands**."   2nd Timothy 1:6

- "Hold fast the pattern of sound words which you have **heard from me**..."   2nd Timothy 1:13

- "And the things that you have **heard from me** among many witnesses, commit these to faithful men..."   2nd Timothy 2:2

- "But you have carefully followed **my doctrine**, manner of life, purpose, faith, longsuffering, love, perseverance, persecutions, afflictions, which happened to me at Antioch, at Iconium, at Lystra ..."   2nd Timothy 3:10-11

All of these readings reflect the time of hiding for Timothy, the time of following Paul. Because Timothy was faithful in the few things, his time of the many things came.

I recall the struggle I had with the Lord over my calling. My heart was in the church and in the kingdom of God, but I saw myself as an evangelist, musician, preacher, or teacher. I saw myself traveling to churches and to the nations, even willing to live by faith, but I was not willing to be a pastor. I would say to the Lord: "I give you my life, I am yours, use me however you would like except as a pastor." I did not want to suffer what I saw my father suffer as a pastor. Finally, one afternoon in my house, alone, hearing a recording of a hymn The Fields Are White For Harvest, the Lord conquered me. I surrendered completely to Him, without reservations or conditions; I took away all restrictions to my surrender and gave the Lord a blank contract for Him to fill. I said, on my knees and crying: "Even if you want me to become a pastor, I will do that until the last day of my life, and I will do it effectively and with joy."

A week later, my father called me and said: "I need you as an assistant pastor in the church in Loiza." At that time, my father was the pastor for two congregations. The main church was in a neighborhood in the town of Loiza, called Mediania Alta, and the second church was in the center of the town in Loiza. At that time, the church in Mediania was beginning to grow in every way. It was in a revival and experiencing a great visitation of the Holy Spirit. The church was going through a period of spiritual renewal. There was fervor in the brethren, baptisms of the Holy Spirit, gifts at work, a cry out to the Lord, and prayers in the early morning.

This movement changed the way we praised and worshiped God; we participated in worship with our entire body and with instruments of all types. There was a zeal for evangelizing and testifying in the streets. The church building fell short in size for the hundreds of people who began to arrive. To secure a seat, you had to arrive an hour before the services started – and I am referring to the prayer services on Mondays. We would begin the services by saying the names of the people who had converted during the day. Lives would convert before the preaching and even after the service had ended. There was joy, happiness, and great expectations. My wife Loyda and I were part of that revival and we were helping my father in the ministry.

It is in the midst of that explosion of power that my father asks me to go – on Sundays and on Monday nights – to help him pastor the second church. Let me tell you this group was completely the opposite of the first. Nothing was happening there; on Sundays, there were some thirty people, and you would not see them again during the rest of the week. Even more, the congregation was very conservative in its liturgy and had no plans of changing.

My father went on Sunday mornings to this second church. In the evening, he would go to Mediania, the main church, to teach Sunday school and celebrate the evangelistic service in the evening, while the second church remained closed.

Several laymen leaders of other Baptist churches would ask my father to lead the services in the evening in the second church, but after several months, they would return to him and resign because they would not see any progress or interest from the members themselves to support the services. Attendance on Sunday and Monday nights did not go beyond five people and their attitude was not the best. In fact, the nickname the second church came to have in the town was the church of the "four cats," a Spanish idiom used when referring to a small group of people.

It is within this context of the second church my father sends me to minister. I had to leave the environment of revival and the joy of my mother church to go pastor the second church that was like the "valley of dry bones." Everything took place exactly one week after my unconditional and without reservations surrender to the Lord. If my father had asked me to pastor a week earlier, my response would have been no. But God had prepared my heart, and so I accepted the call.

My time of the few things began in that place. While the mother church was in revival, different preachers would visit, and everyone would speak of what happened there, I had to go alone and minister to the small church. I say alone, because not even my friends or my wife wanted to go there on a consistent basis. They would go sometimes to fulfill their duty. I now understand it was God's plan because it was my time of anonymity, of being in hiding, of my desert, and of solitude with God. God wanted to try my faithfulness and my vocation in the few things. So I kept at it week after week, month after month, year after year. Sometimes I would go to the service crying and would leave the same way. It was as if nothing was happening. All of this moved me to pray, to fast, and to seek more of God.

One night I arrived first before the person in charge of opening the church. I opened the doors in pairs, and I opened the windows; there were twenty in all. I turned the lights and sound equipment on. Then I began to play the organ with hymns of praise and victory.

When the person in charge of opening and closing the church for the service arrived, he was not only surprised, he was upset. Up until that day, we had celebrated the service with only one of the doors and two or three windows open, with a couple of lights on and without the sound equipment since the service was just for the four or five of us. The person in charge would say: why go through all the trouble? He would come because it was his responsibility to open and close the church, but he wanted to leave as soon as possible after the service was over. I told him: "brother, from today on we will do it this way, with the doors and windows open, the lights, sound, and music on, because something powerful will happen here and I believe it now. The first ones who need to believe that something will happen have to be us. Don't worry though, that I'll take care of closing the windows at the end."

We had many experiences there, the topic of another book about the pastoral calling; but I want to tell you that two years later from that day, the church had an explosion. The prayer circle on Mondays grew to some hundred people and some fifteen youth accepted the Lord, which at that time was very significant. We organized a youth group. I showed one of them to play the organ and he became the first organ player, product of the same church. Then there was music every night. There was both numeric and spiritual growth. The atmosphere and attitude of the people had positively changed.

After some time my dad became ill and decided to resign from one of the churches, since both were now growing and demanded a lot of work. He decided to stay as pastor of the second church, the one I was working in, and to resign from the main church. Several months later, the main church calls me to become their senior pastor. After praying, they decided to select me based on the work realized in the second church. God took me once again to the mother church that I loved so much after my time of the few things. I was a pastor there for ten years until the time the Lord sent us to the United States to pastor in the state of Massachusetts, in the Pioneer Valley, in the city of Springfield where we have been for the past twenty years. Glory to God!

I would add that when the Lord moves us to the city of Springfield, again He sends me back to the time of the few things. At the time we were considering coming to Springfield, I was being called by three large churches in Puerto Rico in addition to a Hispanic church in Connecticut to become their pastor. Compared to those churches, the church in Springfield was smaller and of lower apparent possibilities. It was another second church of Loiza.

As I mentioned earlier, I counted on nineteen members. The church did not have its own facilities, offices, telephones, and front sign; though it did have an abysmal fiscal deficit. There, in that frigid basement in the winter and oven in the summer, I returned to the school of the few things and to the hidden place.

Once again, we embarked on being faithful in the few things; of giving our best and endeavor day-by-day, believing He that called us would support us. Almost seven years went by without being invited to preach to any church or activity, with the exception of a few local commitments. It was a difficult time, and one without recognition.

However, the church began to grow in every way and the experience of the second church in Loiza repeated itself. All of the sudden, doors opened to preach in Puerto Rico and later in other nations. Opportunities arrived to preach in other churches, small, medium, and large churches, in conventions, and conferences. Later the church in Springfield receives its calling to go to the nations and we begin ministries in countries like the Dominican Republic, Peru, Puerto Rico, and Argentina, as well as helping other ministries in Cuba, Ecuador, and Honduras.

God has worked so surprisingly in my life that the vision that burned in my heart to preach the gospel to the nations is now happening some twenty years later. Now the Lord has given me the blessing of carrying out an apostolic ministry and to care for over 40 pastors, 17 churches, and other affiliated ministries.   The promotion came, based on the principles I share in this book, but especially because of the principle of being faithful in the few things; persevering for the entire time the Lord so decides.

My dear brother or sister, wait for your time in the Lord. Never go back, but do not get ahead of yourself.

My Prayer

Lord, I ask you help the readers be faithful in the level they are in now and that they may understand their promotion depends in their faithfulness in the few things. That they not only trust in their talents and gifts, but also in their capacity to be faithful. That they might be able to maximize their time in anonymity, their time in the few things, in their desert just as David did. We rebuke all spirit of envy, conflict, and criticism against those who are also in the process of advancement.

I ask you help them do, in an excellent way, that which they have been entrusted with; that they do everything with thanksgiving. That they could enjoy their time as the Elisha, Timothy, and Joshua. That they might be faithful in the few things during the entire time necessary so they may set lose their promotion. In Christ Jesus, we pray. Amen.

My Prophetic Declaration

- I declare I will be faithful in my time of the few things and I will use this time to focus on what I have been entrusted.

- I declare I will do what I have been entrusted to do with excellence and will do it well even if no one notices.

- I declare that if in the few things I am faithful, when the time comes, I will be put in the many things. My promotion depends on my faithfulness and in my behavior in the few things.

- I declare I will not feel pressured nor relegated by my time of anonymity; on the contrary, I will put that time to produce for my favor. I will learn everything I need to learn. I will serve whomever I need to serve, and I will help others reach their next level.

- I declare I will be like a David, Joshua, Timothy, Titus, or an Elisha; people who did not despise their time in the few things or being behind the scenes. I declare, as they did, when my time comes I will rise to my new level because if I can be faithful in the few things, then I will be put over the many things.

HUMILITY

CHAPTER 12

"Therefore humble yourselves under the mighty hand of God, that He may exalt you in due time".

1st Peter 5:6

Another key element to consider if we are to move to new levels, is humility. John Haggai, when speaking about leadership says that "contrary to what many think, humility gives tensile strength to leadership."[32] There is a great difference between a humble person and an arrogant or prideful person. Humility opens divine doors, pride closes them. Humility releases divine promotion, while pride brings degradation and disgrace. In the Kingdom of God, it is not the same thing to be a humble person than a prideful one. Consider these biblical passages.

- Psalm 138:6 declares that God looks upon the humble, but the proud He knows from afar. Obviously, there is a great difference.
- Apostle James says that God resists the proud, but gives grace to the humble (James 4:6). Again, there is a great difference between being resisted and receiving the grace or favor of God.
- King David also knew the benefit humility brings. He wrote in Psalm 51:17 that a humble and contrite heart, God would not despise. God will never overlook a person who is humble. Being humble pays off.
- In the key verse for this chapter, the Apostle Peter teaches that God will only exalt or promote people who have humbled themselves under the mighty hand of God (1st Peter 5:6).

> **Every promotion and advancement in the Kingdom of God is linked to humility.**

Humility makes God pay attention to you, releases his grace, keeps you from being ignored, resisted, or rejected by God, and provokes, in its due time, God to promote you. Humility precedes every divine promotion. If a person is conceited, prideful, and arrogant in the few things, imagine how much more he will be when given much. No one will resist him.

Humility

We should clarify the term humility, as it does not seem to have the same meaning to everyone. Many people associate humility with poverty, scarcity, misery, backwardness, lack of education, and being constantly under the attack of the enemy. People think that to be humble is to be the devil's punching bag. They think that the worse things go for them, the more humble they will be. However, humility has nothing to do with that. I know people who qualify for the title of humble, according to such a criteria, who are arrogant and prideful. I also know people who have wealth and live in true humility and simplicity.

King David was a humble man and sensitive to the presence of the Lord, and he also was a rich man. An individual's economic condition or social position does not define his humility. In order to be humble you do not have to take a vow of poverty, or accept whatever comes your way as a given. Likewise, to be secure in who you are, have an assertive personality, goals of excellence, good taste, and be in a good financial status, does not necessarily make one a prideful person.

For me, humility begins when a person recognizes the sovereignty and power of God; that God is the great one and it is not him. If a person acknowledges and knows very well within that God is the author of all salvation, that all blessings come from His hand, that without Him nothing can be, and that the Lord is her strength and reason why she is still standing in spite of so much opposition; then we can easily declare there is humility in that person.

> "For by Him all things were created ... all things were created through Him and for Him. And He is before all things, and in Him all things consist."
>
> Colossians 1:16-17

The humble person recognizes that the one sitting on the throne is God and they are at His feet. He recognizes that Jesus is the Lord (Adonai, Kyrios) and he is His servant. The humble person has no problems in giving the glory to God and does not think of himself or herself as self-sufficient. They know everything is through grace, though that does not mean they cannot recognize their own gifts, resources, and accomplishments.[33]

In contrast, the prideful and arrogant person claims the glory for himself at the expense of God. He is constantly talking about how intelligent, virtuous, and capable he is. He keeps exalting himself all the time looking to be recognized. It is important for such a person that everyone knows his accomplishments and recognizes him.

Pride and arrogance are dangerous, because God does not deal with the arrogant or with anyone who takes the glory that only belongs to Him.

Nebuchadnezzar

Look what happened to King Nebuchadnezzar when he claimed the glory at the expense of God.

> "At the end of the twelve months he was walking about the royal palace of Babylon. The king spoke, saying, 'Is not this great Babylon, that I have built for a royal dwelling by my mighty power and for the honor of my majesty?' While the word was still in the king's mouth, a voice fell from heaven: 'King Nebuchadnezzar, to you it is spoken: the kingdom

has departed from you! And they shall drive you from men, and your dwelling shall be with the beasts of the field. They shall make you eat grass like oxen; and seven times shall pass over you, until you know that the Most High rules in the kingdom of men, and gives it to whomever He chooses.' That very hour the word was fulfilled concerning Nebuchadnezzar; he was driven from men and ate grass like oxen; his body was wet with the dew of heaven till his hair had grown like eagles' feathers and his nails like birds' claws."   Daniel 4:29-33

When Nebuchadnezzar took the glory for himself, instead of being promoted, he lost his sanity and descended to the levels of animals and birds. It is very dangerous to take what belongs only to God.

Herod

King Herod also claimed the glory for himself at the expense of God.

"So on a set day Herod, arrayed in royal apparel, sat on his throne and gave an oration to them. And the people kept shouting, 'The voice of a god and not of a man!' Then immediately an angel of the Lord struck him, because he did not give glory to God. And he was eaten by worms and died."
                                    Acts 12:21-23

Herod lost his position, was eaten by worms and died; a very shameful way to die, especially for a king. God changed his royal robes for robes of worms. He immediately rotted. In the end, the prideful will be humiliated and struck by God.

Joseph

Observe the way in which Joseph, when he is before the Pharaoh, gives the glory to God for his skills and gifts, refusing to take any merit for himself.

"And Pharaoh said to Joseph, 'I have had a dream, and there is no one who can interpret it. But I have heard it said of you that you can understand a dream, to interpret it.' So Joseph answered Pharaoh, saying, 'It is not in me; God will give Pharaoh an answer of peace.'"   Genesis 41:15-16

Joseph takes the time to clarify to Pharaoh that if he can interpret his dream, it is not because of his abilities, but by the grace of God. Therefore, it should not come as a surprise that Joseph was later promoted by God to be the Pharaoh's right hand.

Isaac

Isaac did not have a problem identifying the source of his blessing and success. Nor did he have problems declaring it publicly. He did not want other people to be mistaken believing that his prosperity came by his own merits. Truly, Isaac drew his neighbor's attention, when he prospered in the middle of a great drought. Isaac dared to sow in times of drought and obtained a harvest that produced a hundred times fold. On top of that, he was digging wells with great ease and was finding water. Isaac refused to take the credit for his success, and without any problems, he pointed to the One who was the key of his success, God himself.

"And he moved from there and dug another well, and they did not quarrel over it. So he called its name Rehoboth, because he said, For now the LORD has made room for us, and we shall be fruitful in the land."   Genesis 26:22

Truly there is a difference between Herod and Joseph, between Nebuchadnezzar and Isaac. It is not the same to think and act like Herod than like Isaac. There is a great difference between a humble person and an arrogant one.

Humility also includes renouncing your own plans, visions and dreams, in order to accept and flow with the plans of God. It includes recognizing that the plans of God are better than your own. It requires submitting your life fully to the attainment of God's plans for your life.

> Many are stubborn, strong willed, and arrogant;
> even though they recognize the existence of God
> and want His blessing, they insist on doing things
> their own way.

People want to do good things, but in their own way. It has to be how they say it, when they say it; and if is not that way, they get angry. This is pride and arrogance.

Naaman

Remember General Naaman, the Syrian (2nd Kings 5). He wanted to be healed by God, but on his own terms. He did not agree with the treatment or instructions the prophet gave him so that he could be healed; he did not agree with the instructions to go and bathe in the Jordan River, because he wanted things his own way. He had other rivers in mind that were more beautiful and fitting for a man like him. Naaman embodies the typical conduct of a spoiled and prideful human being. It is precisely because of his pride, that the prophet gives him the treatment and prescribes the Jordan River.

Let me tell you again, before you can be promoted or advance to new levels, God will deal with your arrogance, your pride, and with your ego.

> Truly, God has a prophet like Elisha and a river like
> the Jordan to confront our pride and high-
> handedness.

God has to deal with our pride, because He does not want to despise us or look at us from afar. He does not want to demote you to the same level for life, nor have you go through what Herod did. His will is to promote us according to Philippians 1:6, which says: "He who has begun a good work in you will complete it." However, in order for that to happen, He first needs to deal with our pride.

God wants to make sure that when we go higher, are abundantly blessed, at the summit, in the much, that we will know to give him all the glory. He wants us to be the first ones to point to the *author* of our blessing. God does not want us to experiment the syndrome of Nebuchadnezzar or Herod; He does not want our ego to get inflated because of our promotion. There are many who have reached the summit, but have not been able to stay there because the promotion and success have ruined their heart.

The hand of God

Peter clarifies that every promotion and advancement towards a new level comes from the mighty hand of God. The hand that blesses and promotes us is not the hand of men or religious systems, but the hand of God. Many want His promotion in the Kingdom, but seek the favor and affection of men; they are "in the wrong lane." God is not committed to honor or validate what human systems promote without asking Him. God only honors that which He promotes. We need to have revelation of the mighty hand of God.

> **There is a great difference between being promoted by the hand of God and being promoted by the hand of men.**

Nehemiah

Nehemiah had revelation of the hand of God. He personally experienced it and testified about it to the people of Jerusalem. Nehemiah testified it was the gracious hand of God upon him, which gave him the vision of restoring the city. He reiterated that it was the hand of God that gave him grace with the king to get permission, materials, and power; allowing him to transition from a cupbearer to a restoration leader. This is why Nehemiah did not fear confronting neither Sanballat nor his people, because he knew that the mighty hand of God was upon him.

> "And the king granted them to me according to the good hand of my God upon me."
>
> Nehemiah 2:8b

> "And I told them of the hand of my God which had
> been good upon me ..."
>
> Nehemiah 2:18a

Jabez

When Jabez prayed, we not only find him asking for a promotion, but we also find him asking for protection, so that once he ascends to his new level the Lord would keep him from harm.

> "And Jabez called on the God of Israel saying, Oh,
> that You would bless me indeed, and enlarge my
> territory, that Your hand would be with me, and that
> You would keep me from evil, that I may not cause
> pain!"   1st Chronicles 4:10

Jabez is aware that not everyone knows how to manage success. Many let success get to their heads and stop being humble, grateful, and thankful. Many become arrogant and begin to boast about themselves. Everyone should pray each day this same petition: "Lord keep me from harm." Jabez had a revelation about the power that the hand of God has. Jabez prayed the hand of God would be upon him. He knew the hand of God is the one that has the power to bless and nullify every curse. It was the hand of God that had the power to promote him from curse to blessing, from scarcity to expanding his territory, and from being a nobody to being the most important one. Jabez knew what David had declared in the Psalms:

> "You open Your hand and satisfy the desire of every
> living thing."   Psalm 145:16

David

King David also had revelation and experience with the mighty hand of God. He knew the hand under which he had to humble himself and submit. It was not just any hand; he recognized the hand of God and would humble under it. His relationship with the hand of God was so close he composed this psalm exalting its power.

> "Yours, O LORD, is the greatness, the power and the glory, the victory and the majesty; for all that is in heaven and in earth is Yours; Yours is the kingdom, O LORD, and You are exalted as head over all. Both riches and honor come from You, and You reign over all. In Your hand is power and might; in Your hand it is to make great and to give strength to all. Now therefore, our God, we thank You and praise Your glorious name."   1st Chronicles 29:11-13

Nebuchadnezzar

King Nebuchadnezzar finally understood that the glory belongs to God and he rid himself of all pride. After losing his sanity and descending to the level of beasts for quite a long time, he also wrote a psalm:

> "And at the end of the time I, Nebuchadnezzar, lifted my eyes to heaven, and my understanding returned to me; and I blessed the Most High and praised and honored Him who lives forever: For His dominion is an everlasting dominion, and His kingdom is from generation to generation. All the inhabitants of the earth are reputed as nothing; He does according to His will in the army of heaven and among the inhabitants of the earth. No one can restrain His hand or say to Him, What have You done?"
> Daniel 4:34-35

When the hand of God promotes you, who can oppose? Who can prevent it? Perhaps many will not like your divine promotion and your advancement to new levels; perhaps many will not agree, because they do not like you. Perhaps they have reasons to disqualify you, but if the hand of God promotes you, who then may wrestle against the mighty hand of God?

David declared "power and might are in your hand, and **at your discretion** people are made great and given strength" (1st Chronicles 29:12, NLT). Nebuchadnezzar understood that no one could detain the hand of God or question its actions. God does not have a problem exalting whomever he chooses. His hand surpasses every obstacle and every enemy.

If the religious system is the one promoting you, it will have to defend or justify you; but if it is the hand of God, then He will take care of all the details. God honors those he promotes. The key is to make sure that **we humble ourselves under the mighty hand of God.** Our promotion and advancement is found there. Under God's hand, we will receive the adequate and needed treatment before we are promoted. Under his hand, God will deal with our pride, ego, character, ideas, and everything else that needs to be polished, submitted, and consecrated to him.

> **Be careful of every shortcut and of every sensational offer that seeks to exalt you, keeping you from humbling yourself under the hand of God.**

In due time

The main verse for the chapter reminds us again of the time factor. We have to place ourselves under the hand of God for whatever time is necessary. The promise is that in **due time,** he will exalt us. Every legitimate promotion is characterized by having to wait the necessary time. Speaking about the time factor, Pastor Joel Osteen says: "To live your best life now, you must learn to trust God's timing."[34] He adds that we need to guard against being impatient, opening doors by force, and trying to do things with our own strength. It is best to let God do it His way and in his time.[35] Stepping out of the timing (*kairos*) of God is the same as stepping out of the will of God. Let us wait patiently because everything has its time and season under heaven (Ecclesiastes 3:1). Remember: your promotion will come at **His appointed time.** Do not get ahead of yourself. Do not get anxious.

Chapter 12 Notes

(32) <u>Lead On! Leadership That Endures in a Changing World</u> - John Haggai – Word Publishing 1986 (p. 58)

(33) <u>Lead On! Leadership That Endures in a Changing World</u> - John Haggai – Word Publishing 1986 (p. 59)

(34) <u>Your Best Life Now: 7 Steps to Living at Your Full Potential</u> - Joel Osteen - FaithWords 2007 (p. 201)

(35) <u>Your Best Life Now: 7 Steps to Living at Your Full Potential</u> - Joel Osteen - FaithWords 2007 (p. 204)

My Prayer

Lord, deliver me from all arrogance and pride. Help me to understand the great difference between being a humble person and a prideful one. May I always give you glory for everything that I do. Help me to humble myself under the mighty hand of God and wait for my time of promotion. Give me revelation of the power of your hand in order to value it, and receive from it everything that it has to do in me.

Lord, that like Nehemiah, Jabez, Nebuchadnezzar, and David I may exalt your might, majesty, and sovereignty. Help me to die to my grandiose plans, so that I can receive yours and fulfill them in the way that you have chosen.

Lord, deal with my ego, my pride and with every root of arrogance, because I do not want to be struck by an angel, die before my time or lose my sanity. Deliver me from every path that seeks self-promotion and prevents me from submitting myself under your hand. I prefer to humble myself under your mighty hand and wait all the necessary time, because in due time I will be promoted. In Christ Jesus, we pray. Amen.

My Prophetic Declaration

- I declare that I desire to be a humble person and not prideful; that I voluntarily place myself under the hand of God.

- I declare the hand of God is mighty, strong and able to promote whomever he desires.

- I declare I am like Nehemiah, David, and Jabez; who had revelation of the hand of God; they appreciated it, submitted to it, and were promoted to new levels.

- I declare my promotion to my new level derives from a humble heart that is submitted to God.

- I declare I will give glory to God in everything, and like Joseph and Isaac, I will point to God as the cause and reason of my blessing and promotion.

- I declare I will be patient and still, and in humility under the mighty hand of God, because in due time I will be exalted.

TRANSITION
CHAPTER 13

"Why did you come down here? And with whom have you left those few sheep in the wilderness?"
1st *Samuel 17:28*

"You are not able to go against this Philistine to fight with him; for you are a youth, and he a man of war from his youth."
1st *Samuel 17:33*

Sooner or later, when the moment of transition to your new level arrives, you will have to face "Eliab and Saul." They represent the people who seek to stop you at the exact moment of your promotion. They represent those who try to test you or convince you that you neither belong to that new place nor qualify for the same.

The Bible says the Prophet Samuel anointed the young David as the next king of Israel. This anointing began a process of transition in the life of David. The time of anonymity and of taking care of sheep in the desert had finished and would give way to a time of exposure, to a time in the palace. It was a time of transition: first as the musician of the king, then as a troop commander, and finally as the successor to Saul.

One day Jesse, David's father, decided to send him to where the troops of King Saul where positioned for battle, rather than sending him to take care of the sheep as was the custom. Jesse wanted his son David to take provisions to his three brothers who were soldiers in Saul's army and bring news home about their condition. This was a key day for the life of David. God used David's father to propel him to his divine destiny.

It is interesting how God can still use people who do not understand nor support our advance. David had an appointment with Goliath. God had prepared the setting for the transition of David from the few things to the many.

> **God chooses even the enemies you are going to face, since your enemies have the ability to promote you to your new level.**

The giants that come your way are not a simple coincidence; they come your way in accord with the level of promotion God has in store for you. David was moving towards a divine appointment. It was there that a new time of transition would begin towards his true destiny.

When David reaches the camp, he finds all the commotion that Goliath had caused. The giant had challenged Saul and his army to select a brave man to confront him and to decide the battle's outcome based on that confrontation. The story says all the men of Israel who saw the giant fled from him with great fear.

It is in the midst of this situation the young David arrives to his new stage. When David gets word of what was happening, he decides to confront the uncircumcised philistine who had dared to provoke the squadrons of the living God (1st Samuel 17). Then Eliab, David's older brother, upon learning his brother was among them and willing to face the giant tells him:

> "Why did you come down here? And with whom have you left those few sheep in the wilderness? I know your pride and the insolence of your heart, for you have come down to see the battle."
>
> 1st Samuel 17:28

Eliab tried to block David's path. The first thing he tells him is that he has nothing to do or look for there where they were: "Why do you come down here?" He reminds him that his place is in the wilderness. In second place, he tries to minimize and humiliate him; since he tells him his function is insignificant, taking care of a few sheep in the wilderness. In your time of transition, you will be confronted with some Eliabs.

Eliab represents the people who want to guide you and put you in your place, that want to function as your mentor, but lack divine revelation about you. Eliab wanted to return David to the place from where God was taking him. Eliab did not know that the time of the few things, of anonymity, of taking care of the "few sheep" in the life of David was reaching its end. Instead of helping him in his transition to the new level, Eliab becomes a stumbling stone for David. Eliab did not have divine revelation over what God wanted to do with David. He wanted to keep David in a season in his life that had already ended. Eliab judged and tried to intimidate David so he would return to his place. Eliab stands for the people close to you that want to direct and affect your life without any revelation from God about your life. They simply base themselves in your past and in their own understanding.

> **It is dangerous to have people without revelation from God about your life deciding your destiny.**

Eliab also represents those who have failed at the level they are at, who do not do the things they should, and yet they prevent others from rising and doing the work. Do you know people like that?

- They do nothing and they prevent others from taking action.

- They keep themselves from dreaming and do not want others to dream.

- They do not want to work or exert themselves, but they stand against others working.

David was a threat to Eliab because David uncovered and exposed him. David's courage and disposition highlighted the fear and inaction of Eliab. It is disconcerting to see how we can quickly judge the faults of others such as arrogance, malice, imprudence, indiscretion, and at the same time pass right by ours. Eliab was scared to death and in his inner being would have given anything to go to the wilderness to take care of the few sheep of David. However, his pride was not allowing him to accept his reality. Eliab wanted David to leave, but God wanted David to stay.

David was clear about his assignment in that place and he did not allow his older brother to intimidate him. The strategy David used was to **turn from him** (1st Samuel 17:30). He stopped hearing and paying attention to him. Sometimes we are left with no choice other than turning from the people who want to steal our promotion. There are structures, systems, and people who resist change and the only thing you can do is to turn from them. If you do not leave them, they will make you lose your opportunities.

> **It is dangerous to stay taking care of sheep for even one extra minute when it is your season to kill giants. It is dangerous to leave the place God sent you to. It is dangerous to stay next to people who are deterring your promotion, your time for exposure, and your time at the palace.**

Being able to identify the Eliabs that appear in your life and not allow yourself to be intimidated by them is key. Now, it is not easy to fight them, since the Eliabs represent people who are close to you, people you love, who you appreciate, and have authority over you. The Eliabs can be your friends, your brothers, and even your own parents. The more intimate the relationship is, the harder it will be to make your decision to turn from them. However difficult that may be, you should not allow family or close ties to be more powerful and deterministic in your life than the calling and plan God has for you.

Even if it is difficult, you cannot allow them to convince you to return and resign from your new season. It is easy to give in and go back, since the previous level where we come from is well known and mastered; we know what to do there. On the contrary, we are rookies in the new level and there are questions about our ability to triumph. At the same time, we are not welcomed as some see us as intrusive or as a threat.

Identifying and flowing in your time of transition is important so that you do not miss the divine appointment or planned encounter with God. Many fail in their time of transition because they do not know how to manage it. Every period of transition is difficult and complicated as is the transition from childhood to adolescence, from adolescence to adulthood, from adulthood to old age, from being single to married, or married to divorced. It is just as difficult and complicated in the spiritual dimension.

I can imagine the first day Joshua went before the people after the death of Moses or Titus' first day when Paul sent him before the church in Crete. It is possible they had to confront some Eliabs and Sauls, who questioned their place and position. Paul had to reaffirm his spiritual son Timothy when he was left in charge of the church. Paul told him not to let anyone despise his youth and hold him in low esteem because of it. It is almost certain some of the brethren Timothy led were questioning his leadership as they considered him too young. The message they were giving Timothy was return to his few sheep, to his previous level. Nevertheless, Paul's strategy was to strengthen Timothy so that in no uncertain terms would he go backwards, but rather he be affirmed in his new level.

You will not be able to move to your new level if you do not understand the dynamics at play during the period of **transition**. Every person who wants to advance to his new time has to identify and learn to function in his time of transition. Many are confused because they came out of their previous level but have not yet reached or been affirmed in their new level. You no longer fit in the old level, there are no seminars, workshops, or training left for you to take, and you have nothing else to try. On the other hand, you do not yet command the dynamics at work in the new level. Everyone is observing all of your movements and some do not want to give you the space to grow. The transition places you in limbo; you are neither here nor there. This makes you vulnerable because neither of your feet is on firm ground. You were taken from your previous level but you have yet to set your feet in the new level.

David not only had to confront Eliab during his time of transition, but he also confronted King Saul. After David leaves his brother Eliab, King Saul sends for him to learn more about his intentions to face the giant. The first thing Saul tells David is "**You are not able**" (1st Samuel 17:33).

We find in this example another type of person you will have to confront during your time of transition towards your new level, on your way to your promotion, the people who will tell you right in your face "you are not able."

Saul only saw in David an adolescent without military experience. To confront an experienced man of war as Goliath and to defeat him was impossible for all of his soldiers; how much more should it have been for David? Do you know what Saul's problem was with David? Saul could only see David in the physical or natural world and could not see the spiritual level. Fleshy or immature people cannot see the spiritual realm. The Sauls of this world fall short when evaluating you, because their judgment, however sincere, is based only in the natural. Saul could not see the anointing over David because his anointing was spiritual.

Do you remember Gehazi, the servant of the Prophet Elisha, when the great Syrian army surrounded the city of Samaria? The servant could not comprehend how Elisha was so calm when they were about to be attacked. When Elisha tells him: "**Do not fear, for those who are with us are more than those who are with them,**" he was even more confused as he could only see the natural (2nd Kings 6:16). The servant could not see what Elisha had already seen, thousands of angels waiting for their moment of action. Elisha had to pray so his servant would open his eyes and pass the threshold of the natural to the spiritual. Saul was in the same state as Elisha's servant – blind and operating only in the natural dimension.

> **Beware of the Sauls in your time of transition and definitive moment, they can only see and evaluate you in the natural world.**

Saul not only represents blind leaders, but also negative and failed people, people filled with fears and terrors. There are many Sauls nowadays! They are pessimistic and negative leaders who only see the negative, the problems, and the impossible. Beware of people who say you cannot do the things God has said you can do. History showed David could confront and overcome giants.

What would have happened if David had accepted right away the words of the king: "you are not able?" Once we accept we cannot do something, though we might be capable, we will not do it. That is the power of doubt.

King Saul, just as Eliab, was a person of influence and authority in the life of David. We have David confronting Saul, the king, and the experienced captain telling him to his face "you are not able." It is not easy to defy such words and opinions when they originate from a person with authority and experience, from people who are already at the level where you are headed. Once again, we see here the pressure and challenge that is present during a time of transition.

Saul was exercising his position of authority as King of Israel. We know Saul had disobeyed God and had been rejected by God. There are leaders who still maintain their position in the church but no longer have wisdom, power, or anointing. They are dry, bitter, sterile, and empty. The only thing they have is their position. We sometimes see spiritual parents, teachers, pastors, and mentors telling their children "you are not able" basing it only in their own experiences; believing that because they could not achieve certain things, their children will also not be able. The majority of times those "modern day Sauls" do not share their advice with bad intentions, but their words can have the potential of castrating and limiting their children since they transmit their terrors, fears, and failures. Instead of exhorting their children to propel them to their destiny and their new level, they paralyze their children.

It is extremely important that you can see how David confronts the "you are not able" of King Saul. David goes on to explain to the king that his confidence is based on his real life experiences from his previous levels. During his time of anonymity, he became an expert in confronting lions and bears that came to attack his flock. David lived those experiences and was completely sure of his dexterities and abilities.

> "Your servant used to keep his father's sheep, and when a lion or a bear came and took a lamb out of the flock, I went out after it and struck it, and delivered the lamb from its mouth; and when it arose against me, I caught it by its beard, and struck and killed it. Your servant has killed both lion and bear; and this uncircumcised Philistine will be like one of them, seeing he has defied the armies of the living God."
>
> 1st Samuel 17:34-36

David was telling the king that he was not skipping stages or processes, but rather this was his time of promotion, his time of exposure. It is likely David had felt very alone many nights caring for his flocks; but each of those vigils had their purpose in relation to his destiny. It is possible his brothers had felt pity for him to see him alone doing a task of little impact. However, each minute of solitude was preparing him for his time of exposure.

Observe how important this time of anonymity was for David. Encounters with bears and lions qualified him to confront giants. Remember the purpose of your time in the small things, of being in the dark, and in anonymity is to prepare you and equip you for your time of exposure. When that time comes, it will not be necessary for them to know you nor will you need publicity or thousands of people to surround you. At that moment, you will not need distractions but rather you simply need to learn to defeat the bears and lions of that level.

Like David, you need to be certain of who you are, sure about what you have accomplished, and what you have yet to do. David did not hesitate before Saul's declaration nor did he for a moment accept the doubts raised about his abilities. On the contrary, he prophetically announced his victory.

> "Moreover, David said, The LORD, who delivered me from the paw of the lion and from the paw of the bear, He will deliver me from the hand of this Philistine."   1st Samuel 17:37

Confident people will go on to their new level. People who have not skipped processes and have completed their assignments in their previous levels will not return to their "few sheep." Confident and secure people will not allow themselves to be intimidated by those who question or doubt their abilities and calling. Faith and doubt cannot simultaneously operate in a person. Faith will propel you to do what God has enabled you to do. Doubt on the other hand paralyzes you from doing what you would have otherwise been capable of doing.

People full of fear and doubt will never reach nor be grounded in their new level.

Eliab and Saul did not know David was fulfilling a divine appointment; they did not know it was David's time of transition to his new level. But you know what? **David did know. He knew it was his time and that was sufficient.** There are people who want to write your biography without really knowing everything you have gone through. They do not know about your encounters with bears and lions or about your victories over them. They do not know about the treatment God has with you in your time of solitude; they do not know how God is conforming your heart to His and they do not know about the faith lessons you have had in the desert. They do not know that you have gone through the many waters and through the fire; they do not know you have paid the price and that you have patiently and faithfully waited for your time. They do not know this is your time and they will try to lead you astray – some without bad intensions, but others with the worst of intentions and treachery. But the one who needs to know without any doubt when the time has come is you.

> Those who go from level to level are people who are informed about themselves. They know when their season is nearing, they know they can do it, and they flow in their transition.

If you do not know when your time has come or what you are capable of, then when you encounter Eliab and Saul you run the risk of staying in the same level you have always been in. It is dangerous to accept the conclusions of the Sauls of today, because they bring doubt to your life, they paralyze you, they steal your strengths, and without noticing it you will lose your determination.

David had full confidence in the victory God would give him and he was not afraid to confess it. Confident people are easily identifiable in the way they speak and act, not only in front of the Eliabs and Sauls, but also in front of the Goliaths they face.

"Then David said to the Philistine, You come to me with a sword, with a spear, and with a javelin. But I come to you in the name of the LORD of hosts, the God of the armies of Israel, whom you have defied. This day the LORD will deliver you into my hand, and I will strike you and take your head from you. And this day I will give the carcasses of the camp of the Philistines to the birds of the air and the wild beasts of the earth, that all the earth may know that there is a God in Israel. Then all this assembly shall know that the LORD does not save with sword and spear; for the battle is the LORD's, and He will give you into our hands." 1st Samuel 17:45-47

My Prayer

Heavenly father, we come before you in one accord with the reader to ask you to help us identify our time of transition. Let us be able to discern when our time has come to go from bears and lions to giants; to pass from anonymity to the visible place. Help us flow when that difficult time comes in such a way we will not feel intimidated or incapable before the Eliabs, the Sauls, and Goliaths. We do not want to remain our entire lives in a season where we have fulfilled our purpose. Rather, we want to move according to your guidance to the next level.

Help us identify those who want to send us back to the place you took us from. Help us identify those who want to sow seeds of negativity and doubt in us by telling us that we cannot function in the new level. Help us to confront effectively the Eliabs and Sauls, the people who without a complete revelation of our lives attempt to tell us where we belong and what we can and cannot do.

Save us from all fear that may paralyze us and keep us out of the new stage. We set loose confidence over our lives and we say by faith that we can complete the transition to the new level, because we have paid with our time of faithfulness, humility, solitude, and in anonymity. Guide us at all times to take firm steps and move in certainty. In Christ Jesus, we pray. Amen.

My Prophetic Declaration

- I declare it is my time to make the transition to my new season; I reject remaining, receding, or returning to the place from where God has taken me.

- I declare I will have the strength of God to turn away from those who want to send me back to the place from where God has taken me.

- I declare I will have the strength of God to confront those who tell me I cannot do those things for which God prepared me in the previous level. I declare I can do all those things God has told me I can do.

- I declare I will not be intimidated by the Eliabs, the Sauls, or the Goliaths of my new level.

- I declare I am entirely certain I will be able to make the transition – and effectively so – to my new level with the Lord's help.

THE PROFILE OF RUTH
CHAPTER 14

"... Entreat me not to leave you, Or to turn back from following after you; For wherever you go, I will go; And wherever you lodge, I will lodge; Your people shall be my people, And your God, my God. Where you die, I will die, And there will I be buried. The LORD do so to me, and more also, If anything but death parts you and me."

Ruth 1:16-17

The story of Ruth illustrates many of the principles already shared in this book about the challenge of moving from one level to the next. Ruth, the Moabite, exemplifies those who are not willing to stay put where they have been in the past, but who are determined to pay the price to go to new levels. The book of Ruth also narrates the story of another woman called Orpah, who exemplifies those who despise their callings and ignore the opportunities to ascend to new levels in their lives. Such people end up living in the same level and carry out their lives without any mayor transcendence in history.

There are three main characteristics I would like to highlight and share as part of Ruth's profile, a conquering woman who should undoubtedly be part of the profile of anyone who desires to go forward.

1) Ruth was a visionary woman

The first great difference between Orpah and Ruth is found in the fact that Ruth grasped God's vision and Orpah did not. Ruth received a revelation about what God was doing in Bethlehem of Judah and Orpah only received information about the same event.

The passage says that when Naomi became a widow and her two sons died, she decided to return to her homeland having heard the news about Jehovah's visitation and the supply of bread in Bethlehem. Naomi shares the good news and her plans to return to her homeland with her two daughters-in-law. We later find these three women on their way to Bethlehem (Ruth 1:7). Suddenly Naomi reacts, stops, and tells her daughters-in-law that they are not bound to go with her to Bethlehem. Naomi did not have any other sons to offer them and at last, they belonged in Moab, not in Bethlehem. Naomi blesses them, says her farewell (v. 8-9), and leaves. This is where the arguments arise; the daughters-in-law insist on staying with Naomi but Naomi insists on their return to Moab (v. 10-13). Finally, Orpah kisses her mother-in-law and returns to her homeland, to her family, to her culture, and to her gods (v.15). Despite the persistence, Ruth on the other hand, stays firm on her decision and remains with Naomi (v.16).

Ruth was immovable because she had a revelation of her new level, of the new time that was to come. She was able to see, in her Spirit, what lay ahead and understand that it was better than Moab. There is power in vision!

Having vision marks and changes you. Vision directs you and gets you on-track; it gives you power to disassociate yourself from the ordinary, the common, and the comfort zone. The Apostle Paul stated it in an excellent way: when you have seen what is ahead, then you can forget what lies behind and progress to what is next (Philippians 3:13-14). There is a great difference between people who are informed and people with revelation.

A high percentage of Christians walk like Orpah, with information. They file it and forget it. That information does not play a decisive role in their lives; they live their lives as they have lived it in the past. Even leaders, at times, walk based on information and not on a vision. This is the reason why people cannot leave Moab, they do not possess the revelation to understand that Jehovah is visiting their town and bringing fresh bread. Since they have not seen what lies ahead, they cannot proceed and are easily convinced to remain in their present circumstance. **Having vision makes a great difference.**

Although Naomi begged Ruth, blessed her, and kissed her goodbye; Ruth did not leave. Orpah could have even said to Ruth, "let us go back to Moab, there is no purpose for us to go to Bethlehem, our mother-in-law is right." However, Ruth was not moved; she was firm in her decision because she had been marked by the vision of Bethlehem.

> **From a natural perspective, the visionary person can be judged as stubborn but that is precisely where the power of the vision lays: it affects a person in such a way that now they do not have the vision, instead the vision has enraptured them.**

Without that kind of commitment, your vision will not happen because as time passes and obstacles come, you will give up. On the other hand, vision has the power to sustain you; what you have seen in your spirit will set you in motion.

If you would like to go to new levels in your life and your ministry, you must first be marked by vision. For people who go from glory to glory, being a visionary is a fundamental element, not an optional one.

When Ruth had the vision of Bethlehem, her spirit was repositioned to possess those blessings. The principle of the Kingdom of God says that prior to possessing, you must see. You will only possess what you have seen. Seeing precedes possession. This is what God himself taught Abraham.

> "And the LORD said to Abram, after Lot had separated from him: 'Lift your eyes now and look from the place where you are—northward, southward, eastward, and westward; for all the land which you see I give to you and your descendants forever.'"
> Genesis 13:14-15

There is power in vision and that is why the ending of Ruth's story does not surprise me: she marries Boaz, a rich man and owner of many lands. I think Ruth had already seen Boaz in her spirit and that is why no one could make her go back.

Dare to see, dare to lift your eyes. Your vision is waiting for you to adopt it and bring it to pass. Part of the vision's job is to challenge you to move out of the place you have always been in. Once you see what lies ahead, you possess it in your spirit, but then you have to go and step on it and claim it. **Vision moves you to action.**

> "Arise, walk in the land through its length and its width, for I give it to you."
> Genesis 13:17

Warning: Do not ask God for visions if you are not willing to leave your Moab. If you lift your eyes to see the vision, prepare your feet for action.

- When Abraham had the vision, he had to leave his family.

- When Moses had the vision, he had to leave the desert and face the Pharaoh in Egypt.

- When Nehemiah had the vision, he had to leave the palace to go to the city that was in ruins.

- When Gideon had the vision, he had to leave the storehouse where he kept his wheat to go to the battlefield.

- When Paul had the vision in Damascus, he had to stop persecuting Christians to go to the nations proclaiming Christ.

Remember: vision provokes action. If you are not planning to leave your Moab, forget about the vision. Being a visionary is definitely part of the profile of those who go to a new level.

2) Ruth was a woman with aspirations

Ruth was not a common woman; she had aspirations. She had desires, goals, and ambitions. She wanted the best and the excellent; she wanted to progress and prosper. You should understand that when Naomi decides to go back to Bethlehem, it was in hopes of a better livelihood and opportunities. She did not just go to Bethlehem because her family was there and she could receive aid in her widowed stage; she returned because she knew that Jehovah was blessing her hometown once again. Ruth, as well, was not only accompanying her mother-in-law, she went in hopes of better things. I do not think Ruth would have decided to go to Bethlehem to live in the same or worse circumstances than in Moab.

In many Christian circles, aspiring to prosper is seen as sinful. If you even mention it, they begin praying for you so that you will not be damaged or lose your way. Having aspirations is not a sin, wanting to be better than yesterday is not an abomination. Everything depends on what you aspire for. I believe in holy ambitions. In fact, God himself wants us to have desires, aspirations, goals, and ambitions.

"... And the desire of the righteous will be granted."

Proverbs 10:24

"Delight yourself also in the LORD, And He shall give you the desires of your heart."

Psalm 37:4

"Now to Him who is able to do exceedingly abundantly above all that we ask or think, according to the power that works in us."

Ephesians 3:20

David had holy ambitions. He was hungry for the presence of God. He had seen glimpses of the glory of God, but he still wanted more and more of God.

"O God, You *are* my God;
Early will I seek You;
My soul thirsts for You;
My flesh longs for You
In a dry and thirsty land
Where there is no water.
So I have looked for You in the sanctuary,
To see Your power and Your glory."

Psalm 63:1-2

Paul was another man who was hungry for God. He had a revelation from the Lord on the road to Damascus. At one point, he was taken to heaven in a vision; and even then, he still said he wanted more from the Lord. He had holy ambitions.

"And be found in Him, not having my own righteousness, which *is* from the law, but that which *is* through faith in Christ, the righteousness which is from God by faith; that I may know Him and the power of His resurrection, and the fellowship of His sufferings, being conformed to His death."

Philippians 3:9-10

The opposite of having aspirations is being conformed. Orpah, unlike Ruth, was the conformist. Moab and Bethlehem were the same in her eyes; being with or without Naomi, and serving Jehovah or the gods of Moab was also the same in her eyes. Do you know people with that attitude? Orpah was conformed to what she had and where she was.

> **Conformists make a pact with mediocrity instead of excellence, a pact with surviving rather than conquering. As long as they have a roof over their heads, food on the table, and some peace, they are satisfied.**

The Orpahs of today drag their feet to pack their bags. Making the trip and even thinking of moving weighs heavily on them. It is a drag for them to have to start at zero, make new friends, and face new enemies. The price is too high for them; therefore leaving things the way they were is more comfortable. Orpah did not have aspirations outside of Moab. She heard about Bethlehem, but was not enthusiastic about it; she did not have dreams or aspirations. That is why she turned her back to Naomi and to Bethlehem; she turned her back to her new level, to what laid ahead.

A person without aspirations or desires will lose his opportunities. The greater glory that comes from Jehovah is for those who are hungry, not those who are satisfied. It is for those who aspire for more, who desire more, who know there is more, and who know that the best is yet to come. Many will miss a greater glory because they have settled for the glory they are currently experiencing.

Talk to me about your aspirations and desires. For example, where do you hope to be at the end of this year? At what level in your spiritual walk, your family, your finances, and your vocation do you hope to be in five years? What type of inheritance or legacy do you hope to leave for your family, your community, and the Kingdom of God?

If you do not have aspirations or desires, you will permanently reside in Moab, since Bethlehem is the destination of people who want to overcome, who want to advance to new levels, who move in the rhythm of God. If nothing moves you, your Bethlehem will pass you by, because for those who settle, Moab is more than enough.

3) Ruth was a determined woman

An attitude of determination is necessary to go up to the new level. As we have already seen, when Ruth packed her bags to leave towards Bethlehem with her mother-in-law, she was totally determined to be part of Naomi's people and to serve Jehovah her God.

> **Determination releases and achieves things that would not be accomplished any other way.**

Even though Ruth also had the option to return, she did not do it. Naomi did not have anything to offer her. She even tells Ruth that there was no longer a reason for them to remain united. The categorical, certain, affirmative, and determined answer that Ruth gave when Naomi told her she could return to Moab has become one of the widest known verses in Scripture:

> "Entreat me not to leave you, *Or to* turn back from following after you; For wherever you go, I will go; And wherever you lodge, I will lodge; Your people *shall be* my people, And your God, my God. Where you die, I will die, And there will I be buried. The LORD do so to me, and more also, If *anything but* death parts you and me." Ruth 1:16-17

Ruth represents those who are determined and are going towards their new level, while Orpah represents those who are indecisive, ambiguous, neutral, change their opinion, plans, and ideas constantly, and in the end remain in Moab. Do you know people like Orpah? People who when asked to leave, they leave. Orpah represents people who at the sight of a problem, adversity, criticism, or an obstacle, decide to give up on their dreams.

Ruth made one of the best statements of determination that I know of. Even more, not only did she make the statement, she fulfilled it, because Ruth never left Naomi's side.

> **Determined people refuse to step back, they do not go backwards; they are focused on their aspirations and what they are seeking.**

Determined people are like the paralytic of Capernaum. After all the work he did to reach the house where Jesus was ministering, he could not enter it because of the multitude. The story does not end there though. He refuses to return the same way he had arrived and asked to be brought up to the roof, to make a hole on the roof, and to be brought down before Jesus.

I like to have determined people working in my team, people who will break ceilings, who are coherent and true, people who are straight as an arrow. Men and woman who will not shy away when facing difficulties, people who are not tossed around like the waves, and who are not like a vane exposed to the wind.

The first few weeks that Ruth spent in Bethlehem were not easy. She had to deal with her bitter mother-in-law and had to fend for their daily sustenance. Naomi was an elderly widow, and did not have the financial means to purchase food. Ruth asked her mother-in-law to allow her to go to the countryside to pickup grain so they could survive. Ruth could have said, "I came to see you now so you would allow me to return to Moab because I am dying of hunger here." Ruth was determined to triumph in her new level; she was willing to take her blessing by force. Ruth asked Naomi for permission to work on the countryside, from sunrise to sundown. Notice the certainty she had, the vision. She knew the Lord would bring her to a special field where she would find grace (Ruth 2:2). She knew that at any given moment things would turn around to her benefit, which is why she was determined to push forward.

Ruth spoke to Boaz's foreman and asked to be allowed to glean and gather after the reapers, in other words, to gather what the reapers had missed or dropped on the ground. Today, we would call that the leftovers. Ruth was doing a humiliating task even though she had the option to return to Moab. She was determined to take her new time by force so this temporary setback did not bother her. Even more impressive is the fact that she worked hard without rest from morning to sundown (Ruth 2:6-7). Why did she face all this without faltering? Because she was a visionary, she had aspirations, and a firm determination.

> **It is in the midst of adverse circumstances where the determined are separated from the ambiguous.**

Determination and hard work yield results; they bear fruit. In Ruth's case, her hard work and determination set loose God's grace. When Boaz arrives, Naomi's husband's kin, and the owner of the field where Ruth had been working, he inquires about her. Boaz is impressed by Ruth's story, her effort, her work, and her determination. Boaz was impressed by the way the Moabite was fighting to come afloat in her new land, and by the care she had for her mother-in-law (Ruth 2:11). Ruth's determination affected Boaz and freed his favor over her life. It was from that moment forward things began to turn around for Ruth. Take note of this:

- Boaz tells Ruth that she can continue to harvest in his fields (job security).
- Boaz orders his workers not to bother or reproach Ruth (respect).
- Boaz authorized her to drink, as much as she desired, from the water that was only for his workers (advantage).
- Boaz invites her to lunch (preference).
- Boaz orders his workers to no longer do their job fully and let the bundles of grain fall behind on purpose, so that her portion would increase (favor) (Ruth 2:16).
- Boaz blesses her: "The LORD repay your work and a full reward be given you by the LORD God of Israel, under whose wings you have come for refuge" (blessing) (Ruth 2:12).

The rest is history. Because of Ruth's determination and hard work, she becomes the fiancée of Boaz, the prosperous landowner. She becomes the co-owner of all those lands and of course, Naomi benefits and is blessed by being able to live her final years in peace and wellbeing.

There were still more blessings for Ruth, the Moabite, in her new level. Ruth became David's great-grandmother, in other words, part of Jesus' lineage. What an honor for any woman!

> "Boaz begot Obed by Ruth, Obed begot Jesse, and Jesse begot David the king."   Matthew 1:5b-6a

When we read Jesus' genealogy through Joseph, Mary's husband, we find Ruth the Moabite as kin (Matthew 1:5-17).

These blessings were waiting for Ruth and Orpah in Bethlehem, but only one reached them. Only the one who dared to go up to her new level, to pay the price and who was determined never to return to Moab, received the blessing. Ruth knew it would not be easy but that it was possible.

Determined people will break customs, traditions, and rules. People like Ruth will accept the challenge, will be the exceptions, will call the attention of the Boaz's of today and will slip in and reach places where it is said that no one can.

A foreigner, even more, a Moabite was the one who married the rich landowner, entering in the royal lineage of King David and the lineage of the King of Kings, Jesus Christ. People like Ruth will go to new levels and will not lose their destiny or their calling.

My Prayer

Lord, help me like you helped Ruth, to be able to identify the seasons in my life. Help me discern when the time in Moab ends and to be able to make the transition to my time in Bethlehem. I pray that you give me not only the capacity to see what is ahead of me but also to be a person of aspirations. Deliver me from conformism because I do not want to miss my new level. I desire to be a person with goals, and I want to overcome obstacles each day; give me that holy ambition.

Lord, I ask you to help me develop a determined spirit. Take from me all indecisiveness and ambiguity. I pray I will not give up when I am faced with obstacles and criticism; help me to be determined to go forward. Give me the strength to pay the price, to go to my new level, and to my divine destiny. In Christ Jesus, we pray. Amen.

My Prophetic Declaration

- I declare I will not be in Moab a minute longer, because my new level is in Bethlehem.

- I declare that I shake off the spirit and attitude of Orpah. I let go of all spirit of indifference and conformism.

- I declare that like Ruth, I will not go back even though others might ask of me because I have already seen that my best time awaits me in Bethlehem.

- I declare that like Ruth, I will be a person of aspirations, of hope, and holy ambitions because the just shall be given everything they desire.

- I declare I will pay the price and will confront the necessary obstacles striving to move to my new level.

- I declare that I am a determined person and that I will not draw back. I refuse to forsake the blessings awaiting me in Bethlehem.

THE PROFILE OF CALEB
CHAPTER 15

"But my servant Caleb, because he has a different spirit in him and has followed me fully, I will bring into the land where he went, and his descendants shall inherit it."

Numbers 14:24

When we speak of biblical characters that moved to another level, we cannot overlook Caleb, the conqueror. He is one of the few biblical characters who God himself gives testimony of in Numbers 14:24, giving us a clear profile of Caleb: "But my servant Caleb, because he has a different spirit in him and has followed me."

He had a different spirit

Leaders who move on to new levels and decide to follow the Lord and his plans are **people of a different spirit**. When God says Caleb is of a different spirit, He is saying Caleb has a different attitude, a different disposition, another mentality, and is of a different valor; he is different from the rest. God is saying this in positive terms. When God says Caleb has a different spirit, he is obviously comparing him to others. Who are those others? The others are the people Moses was leading to the Promised Land.

Remember the historic moment when God gives testimony of Caleb. The people of God have reached the border of the Promised Land, after being delivered from Egypt, the land of slavery, and having traveled across the desert. They had just finished receiving the report of the twelve spies who had gone to examine the land and whose report set loose a terrible crisis in the camp.

Ten of the twelve spies reach the conclusion it was impossible to conquer the Promised Land. They inform the people there were fruits, milk, and honey, but also that the cities were walled and the inhabitants were giants and well armed. On the other hand, they were inexperienced in warfare, unarmed, and short when compared to the stature of the Canaans.

> "But the men who had gone up with him said, 'We are not able to go up against the people, for they are stronger than we.' And they gave the children of Israel a bad report of the land which they had spied out, saying, 'The land through which we have gone as spies is a land that devours its inhabitants, and all the people whom we saw in it are men of great stature.'" Numbers 13:31-32

The ten spies declared: if we go up, we will die; all of this has been a sham. As they say in Puerto Rico, so much swimming to die at shore. They continued declaring: the wisest thing to do now is to name a new captain to return us to Egypt or we will die in this desert. In spite of the positive and faith-filled report Joshua and Caleb gave, the people preferred to believe the ten spies.

> "Would it not be better for us to return to Egypt? So they said to one another, Let us select a leader and return to Egypt." Numbers 14:3b-4

Of what spirit were the people in the desert? A defeated spirit, one that immediately retreats before the problems and obstacles encountered along the way. Nevertheless, Caleb decided to follow Jehovah and accepted the invitation of God to go up and take possession of the land He was giving them (Deuteronomy 1:20-21).

There is a vast difference between the people and Caleb:

- They were of a backward spirit; Caleb was of an advancing spirit.

- They were thinking about returning; Caleb was thinking about pressing forward.
- They were thinking about Egypt; Caleb was thinking about the Promised Land.
- They were thinking about the kettles of meat they would eat as slaves in Egypt; Caleb was thinking about the delicious and super sized fruits, the milk, and honey of the Promised Land.
- They were thinking about dying; Caleb was making plans to conquer and establish himself in Mount Hebron.

Let me share with you 7 key characteristics in Caleb's profile. He was different from the people, because he first **maintained his good sense and emotional stability.** Folks who are like the people of the desert almost always respond to collective hysteria. If you want to advance to your next level, be careful not to be part of the collective hysteria. This is what happened to the camp. Immediately upon hearing the news from the ten spies, the congregation cried all night, lifted up their voices, complained, disparaged, became depressed, accused Moses, made plans to kill him, substitute him, and return to Egypt.

> "So all the congregation lifted up their voices and cried, and the people wept that night. And all the children of Israel complained against Moses and Aaron, and the whole congregation said to them, "If only we had died in the land of Egypt! Or if only we had died in this wilderness! Why has the LORD brought us to this land to fall by the sword, that our wives and children should become victims? Would it not be better for us to return to Egypt? So they said to one another, Let us select a leader and return to Egypt." Numbers 14:1-4

The scene turned into pandemonium; people did not know their left from their right. When we are hysteric, we lose our perspective, control, and reason. Under those conditions we can do the most stupid and senseless things.

No crisis can be resolved by creating more problems. We need to keep our peace and good sense if we are to resolve a crisis and confront our challenges. You cannot advance to new levels if you lack emotional control.

Different from the 10 spies, Caleb remained levelheaded before the challenge and obstacles; he was in control of his emotions and of what he spoke. He did not allow himself to fall under the spirit of collective hysteria that reigned in the camp.

Beware of the people who host the hysteria virus. People who can make a small fleeting flame into a fire. Beware of exaggerated people who could pass for theatrical actors; the folks who can make a mountain out of a molehill. There is always around them some confusion, chaos, lack of control, speech without thought, and bad management of the facts and reality. Where there is shouting, crying, complaining, and accusations, something positive cannot be achieved until everyone calms their emotions and exercises self-control.

Keep your peace, your self-control, and your good sense; you will need it to go on to your new level. Be of a different spirit; refuse to respond as the hysteric people did before the ten spies. If you do not believe it, ask Jairus. When he arrived with Jesus to find his daughter dead, he found a house that had turned into the spectacle of the neighborhood. All of the curious, critics, skeptics, and mockers were there. And who were they? They were his neighbors and friends. Before he was able to receive the miracle, before he could go to the next level, Jairus – ordered by Jesus – had to throw those people out of his house, living room, and bedrooms. Jesus knew he needed to change the environment of collective hysteria, of doubt and crying, into an environment of faith.

Secondly, Caleb was different because **he refused to be a victim, and instead declared himself victorious.** In the midst of the challenge he encountered, he decided to be victorious while the people decided to be victims. You will never be able to advance to your next level by playing the victim. When you play the role of victim, you expect others to do things for you or on your behalf while you assume the role of impotent, submissive, and passive, putting all responsibility on others.

Crying, complaining, accusing, and self-pity do not resolve problems. The people began to say "poor us and our children, Moses fooled us, we were so foolish to believe him, and God has left us." In fact, they were lying and exaggerating because they had seen the glory and signs of God during those last months. Nevertheless, that is part of the techniques used by those who exploit pity and carry out their lives as victims. They live off deceit, lies, and by manipulating facts. Caleb did his part and assumed responsibility, positively confronting the crisis. People who begin to deceive others and lie when confronted with challenges, and at the same time begin to say they cannot do it, they do not know, and they do not have; **such people will never move to new levels**. Be careful not to fall in the position of victim and beware of walking with people of that spirit.

> **If you are in Christ, you are not a victim you are a victor. You are more than conqueror.**

We continually declare in our church in a high voice and with conviction this prayer: "I am everything the Lord has said I am, I can do all things the Lord has said I can do, and I possess everything the Lord has said I can possess."

You will never reach new levels if you devote yourself to blame everyone else for each challenge, problem, or difficulty that comes your way. Be of a different spirit and stop accusing others. The other response the people gave before the crisis was to accuse God, accuse Moses, and accuse the two spies. There are people who each time they confront a problem or crisis, become frustrated and blame others. They blame their father because they were abandoned in their childhood. They blame the neighbor, a teacher, or the government. They continuously exploit their history with the end goal of avoiding any responsibility. But that is an overused excuse and you are better off healing from those wounds and moving on. Caleb was of a different spirit because he was careful not to fall in the trap of accusing others and avoiding his responsibility.

Caleb was different from the people, because, in the third place **he was a visionary.** Caleb was a visionary that could see what the other spies did not see. What really stands out for this visionary man is that Caleb dared to dream in the midst of giants and walls. In the midst of the attitude of the other spies who were saying: "this is an impossible mission, let's get out of here or we will die," he fell in love with Mount Hebron, he stepped on it symbolically, and declared that it would be his and of his descendants. He pictured himself there building his house and playing with his grandchildren. He asked God for it as his inheritance while the others were making plans to return to Egypt.

> "Except Caleb the son of Jephunneh; he shall see it, and to him and his children I am giving the land on which he walked, because he wholly followed the LORD."   Deuteronomy 1:36

Let me say it once more: people who move to new levels are visionary people. Do you dare to have visions in the midst of your adversities, even in your midnight hour? Anyone can have visions during a glorious service, with two or three anointed prophets prophesying over their life, but to have visions in the midst of adversity and the impossible is another matter altogether. When the entire people of Israel decide to turn back, we see Caleb drawing up plans for his house on Mount Hebron, stepping on his property, and enclosing his land. Oh, thanks be to the Lord for the power of a vision! For that reason, God had no other alternative but to give Caleb what he saw, stepped on, and claimed as his.

He was different from the people in the fourth place because **Caleb made positive confessions with faith.** Caleb confessed and spoke positively in the midst of the crisis. He and Joshua said: "Let us go up at once and take possession, for we are well able to overcome it ... for they are our bread ... and the LORD *is* with us" (Numbers 13:30 & 14:9). People who advance to new levels are those who know to confess well. What you say is important and decisive, because there is power in your tongue; there is life or there is death. What you say will be what you receive, and it will show.

The rest said, it is impossible to go up to the land, and they did not go up. They said, we will die in the desert, and so they died. Joshua and Caleb said, we can; and they did. They said, we will go up and take the land, and they went up. What are you speaking in the middle of your crisis, in the midst of your giants, and in the middle of your Jericho? Are you saying: I didn't know this could happen; it's too good to be true; I can no longer take it; I'm dying here, this is impossible; take me out of my misery, I want to die? Jesus teaches us the opposite. He taught us to speak to the mountains (the obstacles); to order them to move. He taught us to speak to the barren fig tree so it would wither away. He taught us to speak to the winds so they would be silenced and to the sea so it would calm down. Remember what the Prophet Joel taught: "Let the weak say, 'I am strong.'" (Joel 3:10) Continually revise your vocabulary and verify if you are speaking the promises of God; if you are speaking the *rhema* and prophetic word that you have received and that the scriptures say about you.

> The people who advance to new levels do not speak carelessly, because they know that what they say can keep them in the desert forever or propel them to their new season.

Caleb was different from the people in the fifth place because **Caleb exalted God in the middle of the challenges and crisis.** He exalted the name and power of God in the middle of the challenge and crisis, while the ten spies ignored God as if they had reached the edge of the Promised Land by their own strength or abilities. The spies quickly forgot the event of the Red Sea; they forgot the water from the rock; they forgot the bread from heaven; they forgot the column of fire and the clouds; they forgot that no plague touched them, that their clothes did not age or their feet swell; they forgot the signs and marvels that God did with them. In contrast to the people, the name of Jehovah did not cease to come out of Caleb's mouth.

Caleb was of another spirit because he did not get spiritual amnesia. Do you know anyone with spiritual amnesia? He knew the God who took them out of Egypt as in the wings of an eagle, would in turn do the same now with the people. Caleb brought to the analysis the name and power of God and he tells them: you have forgotten our great resource. The enemy might be great and large, but Jehovah is with us and they are lost. If God is with us, we will eat them as our bread.

> "If the LORD delights in us, then He will bring us into this land and give it to us, 'a land which flows with milk and honey.' Only do not rebel against the LORD, nor fear the people of the land, for they are our bread; their protection has departed from them, and the LORD is with us. Do not fear them."
>
> Numbers 14:8-9

People who rise to their next level continuously have God in their newscast. They do not exalt their problems, and even less so their enemies. They exalt and praise God and they trust fully in Him.

Caleb reminds them what God had done in the past and tells them He will do the same now. In the middle of adversity he does not complain nor speak negatively; even less does he accuse God, but rather he exalts and worships Him. He puts into practice the teaching of Psalm 34:1: "I will bless the LORD at all times; His praise shall continually be in my mouth." Now I ask you, are you exalting God in the middle of your transition, now that you are at the frontier of your new level, of your new season? The people of a different spirit praise God when they are facing their giants and their walls. Beware of the people who glorify their obstacles and suffer from spiritual amnesia.

He was different from the people, in the sixth place because **Caleb was a motivator.** Caleb was of a different spirit, because in contrast to the ten spies who dedicated themselves to sowing doubt and mistrust to steal the faith and hope of the people, Caleb devoted himself to motivating others to rise to their new level. The people who go to new levels do not want to go alone; their desire is for others to rise. That is why they concern themselves with motivating, inspiring, teaching, and correcting others so they do not stay relegated or demoted. Joshua and Caleb were compelled to motivate the people and transmit their faith unto them, because they also wanted the people to take possession of their inheritance; that they might go up to their next level. Do not despise nor overlook people of faith, people who seek you out to propel you to your next level, who come to motivate, challenge, inspire, encourage, and tell you that you can do it. Open your ears; do not let the murmuring of obstinate people or the noise of their tongues impede you from hearing your Joshua or your Caleb.

Nowadays we live in a negative and individualistic society. Caleb did not only think about himself and his descendants, he thought about the people. He preoccupied himself with the people to such a degree that he nearly died from being stoned. How hard it is to motivate and inspire most people to develop their potential, to be blessed, and to progress. But how easily are the same people dragged by negative influences; they believe them without question and they flow with them.

> **People who go to new levels are not dragged along by negative influences because they can recognize their Caleb and do not allow him to pass by unnoticed.**

Caleb was different from the people because in the seventh place **Caleb decided to follow Jehovah independently**

of the majority rule. In the decisive moment, Caleb decided to believe God and to follow him. Caleb did not allow the ten spies or the multitude to influence him in the decision to follow the Lord. All of the people, thousands of them, decided not to go up and follow the Lord; only two decided to go up, only two decided well.

Following the Lord is not a question of polls and surveys, but one of faith. There are people who decide based on what most people do, **but the majority can be wrong and misguided.** This has been proven throughout history. The important thing is to decide to do what is good and not what the majority chooses. Remember what you are seeking is not to be in good terms or to be popular with the majority, but rather to decide well and in doing so move forward to your new season. The great challenge in life is to decide well in the defining moment; because there lays your blessing, your progress, and your victory. Examine your criteria for making decisions.

In spite of the terrible pressure Joshua and Caleb experienced, they did not yield or change their decision. In that moment, they decided to go up. Deciding to follow the Lord was to become part of the minority; it was to become discredited, exposed to ridicule, rejection, and even death. There are many people who having decided well, change their decision when pressure, criticism, and rejection come their way.

Caleb remained firm because he was of another spirit. He did not respond to pressure, fear, danger, to the loss of prestige, friendships, nor even the loss of his own life. He did not change his decision. History demonstrates he decided well, while the rest died in the desert. Caleb survived and entered the Promised Land.

> **People who rise to new levels are not afraid to make the right decision, independently of the opinion of others. They do not fear following God and believing Him even though the majority decides to do the opposite.**

People of a different spirit do not fear having to make decisions and decide well. They do not live from polls or surveys, but rather through revelation, wisdom and conviction. Caleb knew there was no way they could lose if he decided to believe God. People who move on to another level believe God. They believe God can do everything He has promised and He can do things even more abundantly than what we have believed or thought.

The biblical passage of this story says God was provoked by seeing so many incredulous and inconsistent people, people with spiritual amnesia; so much so that He resolved to eliminate them once and for all. The latter did not take place thanks to the intervention of Moses.

> "Then the LORD said to Moses: How long will these people reject Me? And how long will they not believe Me, with all the signs which I have performed among them? I will strike them with the pestilence and disinherit them …"   Numbers 14:11-12

In contrast to the people, God was pleased with Caleb because he believed God and decided to follow Him, at whatever cost. For this reason, God himself took charge of Caleb's promotion to his new level. While He told Moses the current generation would not go into the Promised Land and instead would go in circles in the desert until their death; He said He would bring Caleb into the land where he had gone and He would give Caleb and his descendants what he had claimed, Mount Hebron.

> "Because all these men who have seen My glory and the signs which I did in Egypt and in the wilderness, and have put Me to the test now these ten times, and have not heeded My voice, they certainly shall not see the land of which I swore to their fathers, nor shall any of those who rejected Me see it. But My servant Caleb, because he has a different spirit in him and has followed Me fully, I will bring into the land where he went, and his descendants shall inherit it."
> Numbers 14:22-24

> People who move on to new and higher levels are like Caleb, of a different spirit, and God will not overlook them. Caleb was not the exception; everyone who decides for God will be brought to his or her next level by Him; God himself will take charge of giving them their Mount Hebron.

If you have read this book until here the last chapter, it is because you are truly interested in advancing to your new level, to your new time, and to your new season. I ask you: how many of the characteristics that we found in the profile of Ruth, of Joshua, and of Caleb are in you right now? Take some time to examine yourself, because to move to your new level you will have to be a Caleb, a Joshua, a David, or a Ruth of this age.

I await you at your next level. See you at the top.

My Prayer

Lord, we want to be of the spirit of Caleb, we want to decide to follow you at all times. Help us always to obey you, especially during times of transition, change, and challenges. Give us the faith, valor, and determination of Caleb so we do not yield to the pressure of those surrounding us who decide to go backward instead of advancing.

Keep our ears from being contaminated with their complaints, accusations, and plans to go back. Keep our thoughts so we do not speak negatively or contradict what you have already said. As Joshua, help us enter the Promised Land, our next level. We want to set foot on it, claim it, and live in it. We reject going back to Egypt or dying in the desert. We do not resign from our inheritance, but rather we claim it and desire to pass it on to our descendants. We claim our Mount Hebron and we will not leave it in the hands of our enemies. As Caleb, I confess you are with us and with you, we are more than conquerors. In Christ Jesus, we pray. Amen.

My Prophetic Declaration

- I declare that as Caleb, I will be of a different spirit; I will be different from the generation of the desert. I will not retreat before the challenges and difficulties of life, but rather I will go up and advance.

- I declare that as Caleb, I will keep my good sense, my peace and objectivity before the dangers and challenges I have to confront in route to my new time. I will not respond to collective hysterias or dwell in environments of confusion and negativity.

- I declare that as Caleb I will not adopt a victim mentality or confront my challenges maximizing self-pity. I refuse to remain passive or paralyzed before the challenges waiting for someone to do something for me. I am not a vic ... tim, I am a vic ... tor.

- I declare that as Caleb I will dare to have a vision in the middle of adversities. I will dare to dream of my new level and I will dare to claim it even in the midst of people who say it is impossible. I am a visionary; I am connecting with my future.

- I declare that as Caleb, I will speak as a person of faith and I will not speak carelessly since words have power of life or of death. I will speak what God has already said that I am. I can realize and carry out things according to his word, his promises, and his calling for my life.

- I declare that as Caleb, I will exalt God in my challenges. I will not exalt the problems and even less my enemies. God will be in my news; I will not forget His powerful wonders of the past since His power never diminishes. He opened the way where there was no way and He will have no problems doing it again. The good work He began in me will not be left unfinished, but rather He will perfect it.

- I declare that as Caleb, I will be a motivating agent for my family and those who surround me. I will tell them with all my heart to rise and go up so that together we can move to the new levels God has for us.

- I declare that as Caleb, I decide to follow God. I choose to believe God and I decide to obey him. Even if no one else decides to follow God, I will go because there is no way I can lose if I go after God. My divine destiny is not to die in the desert on the edge of my new level; my destiny is to go up and take possession, advance, and conquer. Amen.

CONCLUSION

Dear reader, let me say it one more time: it is your time to arise; it is your time to embark on your progress to your new level, because your new season has arrived. Loosen yourself of all inertia and conformism, let go of all excuse and reasoning, and be free of all fears and terror.

It is time to climb

It is time to say goodbye to Egypt, to the desert, and Moab. It is time to cease sitting next to things that are dead, to sterile traditions, to customs that are good but cannot impact our destiny.

It is time to cross our Jordan

Listen to this: the best for your life is yet to come and is ahead for you. There is still a road, a journey, to be travelled. Please do not hold back, do not give up but rather press on! Do not allow your past, your adversities, or your failures to deprive you of going to new levels in your faith and in your calling.

It is time to break the circle

Do not spend time in one more roundabout or circle in the desert; break that vicious circle and march ahead. It is a new day, it is your new sunrise, it is the day of your promotion, and your new season has arrived.

It is a new season

Receive the Shulamite's song and make it your own.

"The voice of my beloved! Behold, he comes leaping upon the mountains, skipping upon the hills. My beloved is like a gazelle or a young stag. Behold, he stands behind our wall; he is looking through the windows, gazing through the lattice. My beloved spoke, and said to me: 'Rise up, my love, my fair one, and come away. For lo, the winter is past, he rain is over and gone. The flowers appear on the earth; the time of singing has come, and the voice of the turtledove is heard in our land. The fig tree puts forth her green figs, and the vines with the tender grapes give a good smell. Rise up, my love, my fair one, and come away!'"   Song of Songs 2:8-13

Speaking prophetically, we know the times ahead for our nation and the rest of the world will be critical. The Apostle Paul called them "perilous times" (2nd Timothy 3:1). Our Lord himself taught us regarding the final times (end of the ages) and left signs to help identify them. His teachings indicate that in these times, the love of many will grow cold and lawlessness will abound. However, paradoxically, they can also be the best times for the church to fulfill its calling and commission. It is for that very reason that the church has a message of faith, hope, healing, and restoration. A message that is constantly becoming more pertinent and accessible to a world that is hurt, beaten, and powerless.

However, for the church to maximize this great, and perhaps last, chance to realize its mission, it has to be a church that is alive, powerful, active, and moving from power to power and glory to glory. It cannot be a conformist church, one that is passive and filled with religiosity, living according to the pattern of the world. Instead, it needs to be one that is living according to the principles of the Kingdom. I am talking about a church that has risen up, crossed the Jordan, expelled the enemies, and divided its inheritance; a renewed church, which leaves its four walls and comes out of hiding, and assumes a role of leadership and influence. I speak of a church that walks according to biblical standards and under the guidance of the Holy Spirit, with all the gifts, resources, and assets activated, and with an apostolic and prophetic government that transforms the nations and changes generations.

The Lord spoke to Israelites in their time of captivity and exile amid gloom and darkness saying, "Arise, shine; for your light has come! And the glory of the LORD is risen upon you." Now I can see that these words are being fulfilled in the church and the leadership of this new century.

I see leaders who rise up and move the church to new heights of glory, grace, and effectiveness. They are leaders who receive divine strategies and leave their four walls. They discard small or limited mentalities, old patterns, and archaic and ineffective methods. They are leaders who left behind poverty and false humility, religious legalism, and debauchery, to become men and women in the style of Joshua and Caleb who are visionary, bold, daring, and faithful. I see leaders who have gotten up, shaken themselves from their fall or from simply laying down passively, and have undertaken and overcome obstacles. Leaders committed to achieving the vision and purpose that God gave them.

We need to continue praying for an awakening of our current leadership and developing a conscience of renewal, of change, and of updating that is so needed in the leadership and the church. We need to train those pastors and leaders who are tired of being in the same place and of working with little results. We need to lift up a new generation of leaders who will take the reins of this century so they may live and reflect the spirit of Joshua and Caleb.

My goal is to continue bringing this message to the different churches in the nations that the Lord has placed under my apostolic covering, in the different gatherings of pastors I may be in, and with the leadership of the church. Similarly, I also seek to orient and educate the new generation of young people.

I hope that other renewed pastors will also become instruments of change. In that direction, I declare that this book will confront the leaders of ministries making them uncomfortable, but also inspiring them to create the attitude and atmosphere needed to initiate or promote change towards new levels, with the objective of maximizing the opportunities the church will have in this new, and perhaps, last century of humanity. Amen.

BIBLIOGRAPHY

- <u>Mujeres de poder (Women of Power)</u> - Silvana Armentano - Editorial Adoradores Unidos
- <u>Walk in God's Pattern for Success</u> - John Bevere - Charisma House 2002
- <u>*Changes* Conference</u> - Alberto Guerrero - Preached at the Samarian Church, Madrid, Spain, 2007
- <u>The Seven Secrets</u> - John Hagee – Charisma House 2004
- <u>Lead On! Leadership That Endures in a Changing World</u> - John Haggai – Word Publishing 1986
- <u>Imitation is limitation</u> – John Mason – Bethany House Publishers 2004
- <u>The Impossible Is Possible: Doing What Others Say Can't Be Done</u> - John Mason - Bethany House Publishers 2003
- <u>Be all you can be!</u> - John Maxwell - David C. Cook Distribution 2007
- <u>Your Road Map for Success: You Can Get There from Here</u> - John Maxwell - Thomas Nelson 2002
- <u>Thinking for a Change</u> - John Maxwell – First Warner Books 2003
- <u>Think on these Things</u> - John Maxwell - Beacon Hill Press 1999
- <u>Journey to Significance</u> – Tony Miller – Charisma House 2003
- <u>The Law of Recognition</u> - Mike Murdock- Wisdom International 1999
- <u>If You Want To Walk On Water, You Have To Get Out The Boat</u>- John Ortberg - Zondervan 2001
- <u>Your Best Life Now: 7 Steps to Living at Your Full Potential</u> - Joel Osteen - FaithWords 2007
- <u>Even As Your Soul Prospers</u> - Thomas Weeks III - Harrison House 2004
- <u>You can reach the top</u> - Zig Ziglar - Cook Communications Ministries 2005
- <u>The Potter's House</u> - T.D. Jakes - TV program, TBN TV 2005
- <u>Prophetic Conference</u> - Héctor Torres – Presented at the Apostolic and Prophetic Conference in Springfield, MA 2007

www.ingramcontent.com/pod-product-compliance
Lightning Source LLC
LaVergne TN
LVHW011222080426
835509LV00005B/273